Beth Robbins

D0165146

Andrew Carnegie Libr.
Livingstone College
701 W. . . . St
Salisbury, NC 2. . .

"Information through Innovation"

Andrew Carnegie Libr...
Livingstone Col ge
701 W ... St.
Salisbury, C 2...

DOS 5

SIMPLIFIED

Rod B. Southworth

Laramie County Community College

Andrew Carnegie Library
Livingstone College
701 W. Monroe St.
Salisbury, NC 28144

boyd & fraser publishing company

Credits:

Acquisitions Editor: James H. Edwards
Production Coordinator: Patty Stephan
Marketing Manager: Christopher Will
Manufacturing Coordinator: Karen Truman
Composition: Alexander Typesetting

 ©1993 by boyd & fraser publishing company
A Division of South-Western Publishing Company
Danvers, MA 01923

Manufactured in the United States of America

All rights reserved. No part of this publication may be reproduced, stored in retrieval system, or transmitted, in any form or by any means, electronic, mechanical, photocopying, recording, or otherwise, without written permission from the publisher.

Names of all products mentioned herein are used for identification purposes only and may be trademarks of their respective owners. South-Western Publishing Company and boyd & fraser publishing company disclaim any affiliation, association, or connection with, or sponsorship or endorsement by such owners.

Library of Congress Cataloging-in-Publication Data

Southworth, Rod B., 1941-
  DOS 5 simplified / Rod B. Southworth.
      p. cm.
  Includes index.
  ISBN 0-87835-943-5
      1. Operating systems (Computers)   2. PC-DOS (Computer file)   3. MS
  -DOS (Computer file)   I. Title.
  QA76.76.O63S598   1993   92-32362
  005.4'46--dc20   CIP

Andrew Carnegie Library
Livingstone College
701 W. Monroe St.
Salisbury, NC 28144

1 2 3 4 5 6 7 8 9 10 MT 5 4 3 2

CONTENTS

PREFACE

DOS 5 Simplified is ideally suited for use in any formal educational or training environment, or for self-study. It was specifically developed with a one- or two-credit DOS course in mind, but it is equally appropriate for use as a supplementary book in any course that introduces DOS commands. Even though no previous experience with DOS is required in order to use this book, students who gain the most from it are those who have already experienced frustration when trying to use DOS effectively.

OBJECTIVES OF THIS BOOK

The objectives of this book are as follows:

- To provide readers with a fundamental overview of the components of personal computer systems.

- To introduce readers to the concepts of using an operating system.

- To simplify the use of those commands most frequently used and their associated options.

- To show how to use both the command line and the DOS shell to execute DOS commands.

- To improve the reader's overall ability to use personal computers effectively through minimized keystrokes, improved disk and memory management, and customized execution of computer processes.

- To give users the necessary foundation to continue learning DOS on their own.

DISTINGUISHING FEATURES

Simplifies Using DOS

In order to accommodate the different backgrounds and levels of expertice of students using this book, topics in this text are presented in a logical step-by-step manner. A summary of objectives is included at the beginning of each chapter. This text's approach, which builds on students' prior experience and carefully constructed examples of DOS in action, helps readers become more self-sufficient personal computer users.

Focuses on Frequently Used DOS Commands

This textbook features step-by-step instruction on the most frequently used DOS commands and their associated options. It is designed to help readers gain better understanding and control of personal computers through the efficient use of DOS.

Distinguishes Between Internal and External DOS Commands

In the early chapters, internal and external DOS commands are covered separately in order to help readers understand the basic differences between these types of commands. Later in the text, DOS commands are presented by functional use.

Covers Hard Disk versus Floppy Disk Environments

In keeping with the current trend in personal computer instruction, this text emphasizes the hard disk environment, but also addresses the floppy disk environment. Examples of DOS commands and lab exercises are given for both environments. For labs using only floppy disks, the Instructor's Manual provides instructions for configuring a floppy disk to imitate a hard disk environment.

Uses the Command Line and the DOS Shell

Knowing how to enter DOS commands at the system prompt is very helpful and often times a necessity for using the DOS shell. For this reason, primary emphasis is placed on entering commands from the command line. Where applicable, command line examples are followed by examples using the DOS shell for comparison. The shell is introduced early in this text. The reader (or instructor) should determine which approach is preferred. The shell is covered in specific sections that can be easily bypassed, if desired.

Emphasizes DOS Structure

An overall understanding of DOS structure is essential for effective computer use. This text's thorough coverage of disk organization and management teaches readers to effectively use computer systems with increased efficiency.

Covers Advanced DOS Usage

The advanced topics in this text include customizing DOS, memory management, and advanced batch files. The advanced DOS commands covered include FASTOPEN, FDISK, MODE, PRINT, SET, SETVER, and SYS.

Features Class-tested Exercises for Floppy and Hard Disks

Each chapter includes a substantial set of student-tested exercises. These exercises build on material learned from previous chapters and include new material from each chapter, as well. Some exercises are included in the body of the text for immediate reinforcement, and others are at the end of each chapter. Each chapter contains separate exercises for both floppy and hard disk systems.

Uses Actual Screen Illustrations

DOS commands are illustrated with screen "dumps" that accurately reflect what users' screens will look like as they execute target commands. The screen illustrations provide users with visual verification, which highlights the impact of each operation performed.

Proven Material

This text has evolved from the collective experience of the instructors and students who have shared their comments and suggestions with the author. Every attempt has been made to preserve the integrity of those elements that proved effective and to improve those that did not.

Instructor's Support Materials

An Instructor's Manual featuring additional student exercises, helpful teaching suggestions; answers to chapter review questions; and a large set of class-tested, multiple-choice test questions is available for use by adopters of this text. Instructors should contact South-Western Publishing Company to request this supplementary material.

ACKNOWLEDGMENTS

This book would not have been possible without the guidance, help, and advice of many supportive individuals. To the many reviewers I offer my thanks for providing valuable contributions during the book's development:

Susan Beal
Louisiana State University

Floyd Leach
University of California at Riverside

Peter Chase
Sul Ross State University

Geetha Murthy
Harper College

Roy W. Hedrick
University of South Carolina

Roger Stone
Northern Montana College

I especially wish to thank Patrice Gapen for her constant encouragement and support. I also wish to thank the students and faculty at Laramie County Community College who had faith in my material and never failed to make valuable comments with regard to what they did and did not like. The entire staff at boyd & fraser, especially Jim Edwards and Patty Stephan, did a remarkable job of editing and producing this book. To all of these people, I remain indebted for their efforts on my behalf.

Rod B. Southworth
Cheyenne, Wyoming
November 1992
Prodigy ID: SPGJ85A

INTRODUCTION TO PERSONAL COMPUTERS

HARDWARE

    The Central Processing Unit (CPU)

    Primary Storage (RAM)

    Input/Output Devices

    Secondary Storage

SOFTWARE

    Application Software

    System Software

Chapter 1
INTRODUCTION TO PERSONAL COMPUTERS

Chapter 1 gives an overview of the basic components of personal computer systems. The term PC, rather than personal computer, will be used in this text. Students using this text undoubtedly have varying degrees of PC experience and knowledge; this chapter provides a common framework of concepts and terminology related to IBM and IBM-compatible PCs.

This chapter covers the two major parts of all PC systems: hardware and software. Having a good understanding of these basics will simplify the learning of DOS, the Disk Operating System for IBM and IBM-compatible PCs.

When you purchase a PC, you may need to make choices about the power of the CPU and the types of input, output, and storage devices to be attached. The technical knowledge presented in this chapter will aid you in making these choices.

HARDWARE

Hardware refers to the physical components of a computer system. Typically, hardware includes four categories: the Central Processing Unit (CPU), primary storage (RAM), input/output devices, and secondary storage devices. Figure 1.1 summarizes the various PC hardware parts discussed in this chapter.

Figure 1.1
PC Hardware

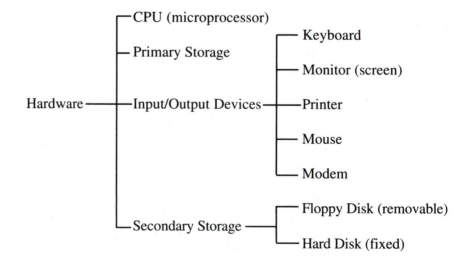

The Central Processing Unit (CPU)

The **central processing unit**, or **CPU**, is often described as the "heart" of a computer system because it controls all activities within the system. The CPU is usually one of four **microprocessor** chips designed by Intel Corporation: the 8088, 80286, 80386, or 80486. Each of these microprocessor chips has different capabilities, related primarily to speed and overall processing power. Future CPUs will use more powerful microprocessors, such as the Intel P5 chip.

All computer circuits, including microprocessors, function in one of two states: on or off. Symbolically, we represent the on condition with the value 1 and the off condition with the value 0. These two values are *binary digits*, or **bits**. Groups of bits are combined to represent characters that we need to store data on a computer. A character is a number (0-9), alphabetic letter (A-Z), or special symbol such as an asterisk, dollar sign, or decimal point. For example, the bit pattern 01000001 represents the letter A.

A *binary item* or **byte** is a group of 8 bits, representing a single character. Many earlier computers were "byte machines." However, it is more efficient to work with more than one character at a time. When bytes are grouped (always in multiples of 2), the addressable groups are called **words**. A 16-bit word represents 2 characters, a 32-bit word represents 4 characters, and so on. Word machines access and transfer characters faster than byte machines. The original IBM-PC, which used the 8088 microprocessor chip, had a 16-bit internal word structure with an 8-bit path for transfer of input and output data. All newer microprocessors have data paths that contain more bits (see Figure 1.2).

All microprocessor chips use a **clock rate** that determines the frequency of the internal operations and keeps everything in proper synchronization. The need for an internal clock is analogous to the need for a conductor at a symphony to control the beat. The faster the clock runs, the faster the computer can process data and instructions. Clock rates are measured in units called **megahertz (MHz),** a term for one million cycles per second. The internal clock speed of the 8088 chip is a relatively slow 4.77 MHz. Figure 1.2 identifies the major differences in commonly used microprocessor chips.

The microcomputer's overall processing capability is directly related to the internal clock speed and the width of the data paths. For example, a 33 MHz 80386DX is roughly 10 times more powerful than the original 8088 microprocessor. The 80286 (or 286 for short) microprocessor suffices for many home applications. However, we need at least the

Figure 1.2

Microprocessor
Chips
in PCs

CHIP TYPE	CLOCK SPEED (MHz)	INTERNAL DATA PATH (bits)	EXTERNAL DATA PATH (bits)
8088	4.77	16	8
80286	8-16	16	16
80386SX	16-25	32	16
80386DX	25-40	32	32
80486SX	20-25	32	32
80486DX	25-66	32	32

processing power of the 80386DX for complex graphics used in desktop publishing or computer-aided design (CAD) applications. Most PC applications are limited not by the speed of the hardware, but rather by the speed of the human sitting at the keyboard. Don't be discouraged if you don't have the latest chip. The 386 and 486 chips, while not as fast and powerful as the P5 chip, are adequate for most applications. Because software continues to make use of faster and more powerful processing capabilities, we recommend that newly purchased systems contain the most advanced hardware the user can afford.

Primary Storage (RAM)

Primary storage is a temporary holding location for both software and the data to be processed. Once software is loaded into primary storage, the programmed instructions can be executed by the CPU. The software tells the CPU the location of the data and the processing steps. The amount of primary storage on PCs typically ranges from 640KB to 4MB. A **kilobyte (KB),** roughly equivalent to 1000 characters, is 1024 bytes. A **megabyte (MB)** is 1 million bytes. Only the 8088 chip in Figure 1.2 is severely limited in memory capacity. Its memory is limited to 1MB.

Because these storage locations are accessible at any time, primary storage is called **RAM (Random Access Memory).** Software and all data must reside in RAM to be processed. Data contained in storage locations remains there until new values replace it, or until the electricity has been turned off. Most RAM chips lose their stored value when power is lost. Thus, primary storage is considered temporary. To permanently save data, you must record it on a **secondary storage device** such as a magnetic disk.

PC users should realize the potential damage that static electricity can do to sensitive electronic circuits. The amount of static electricity that you sometimes feel when you touch a doorknob or another person is many times greater than the static electricity needed to damage a microprocessor or RAM chip. You can minimize the potential for static electricity damage by using a static mat or static strip to discharge static electricity buildup.

Input/Output Devices

Input/output devices are the means by which you enter data into the computer (input) or view previously entered data (output). This section discusses the five most common input/output devices: keyboard, monitor, printer, mouse, and modem.

The Keyboard

The **keyboard** on a PC is an input device similar to a typewriter keyboard, except it has additional keys. IBM-PC and IBM-compatible keyboards typically have more than 100 keys. The placement of these keys varies somewhat among manufacturers. It is important to understand these keys before working with DOS. The four major areas of the extended keyboard are shown in Figure 1.3.

Figure 1.3
Typical Extended Keyboard

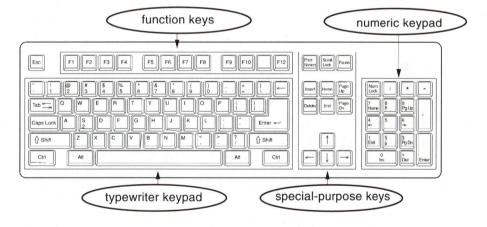

Earlier keyboards have a set of 10 special keys, called **function keys.** These keys, labeled F1 through F10, are located on the left side of the keyboard. Today's extended keyboards have 12 or more function keys located on the top row. Function keys are "programmable" in that they serve different functions depending on how each software program defines their use. When we refer to a function key, it will generally be called by the key name, such as the F1 key or the F6 key. Other times it will be shown inside brackets, such as <F1> or <F6>.

The **numeric keypad** is a group of 17 keys, including keys numbered 0-9, located to the right of the keyboard. The keypad is used to enter numbers when the Num Lock key is on. The Num Lock key is a toggle key, one that acts as a switch. Press it once to switch it on; press it again to turn it off. The light on the Num Lock key indicates it is toggled on for numeric input. Another example of a toggle key is the Caps Lock key. It shifts all lowercase alphabetic characters (a-z) to uppercase (A-Z) when switched on. It only affects alphabetic characters.

You can also enter numbers by pressing the numeric keys located on the top row of the **typewriter keypad,** located just below the function keys. Hold the Shift key down to enter capital alphabetic letters.

The extended keyboard (see Figure 1.3) has **special-purpose keys** that can be used to position the cursor on the screen. For example, pressing the left arrow key one time moves the cursor back (left) one position. The **cursor** is a special character, usually a box or an underline, that identifies a location on the computer screen where the next action or entry of data will occur.

Some keys are pressed in combination with other keys to enter the desired results. Dual-purpose keys have two characters, an upper and a lower character, shown on each key. To enter the upper symbol on a dual-purpose key in the typewriter area, you must hold down the Shift key. Thus, to enter a $, hold down the Shift key and press the 4 key. In addition to the Shift key, the Control (Ctrl) and Alternate (Alt) keys can be used to change the meaning (or use) of certain keys. Some of these combination keys and their functions are shown in Figure 1.4.

Figure 1.4

Combination Keys

COMBINATION KEYS	FUNCTION
Control + Break (Ctrl-Brk)	Cancel (break) the execution of a command or operation.
Control + S (Ctrl-S)	Momentarily stop screen display to allow time to view contents.
Shift + PrintScreen (Shift-PrtSc)	Print current screen contents; must be connected to a printer. (On some keyboards, it is not necessary to press the Shift key.)

As you enter commands from a keyboard, you can use the Backspace key, normally shown as a large left-facing arrow (←) to back up and erase unwanted characters. The **Backspace key** erases one character at a time to the left of the current cursor position each time it is pressed.

Once a command has been keyed completely, it is sent to the computer, or entered, by pressing the Enter key. The **Enter key** is normally located near the right side of the keyboard, just to the left of the numeric keypad. On most keyboards it is shown as a bent left-facing arrow (←). Figure 1.5 summarizes the keyboard keys.

Because modern keyboards are electronic and not mechanical, a very light touch activates the keys. If you continue to hold down a key, the keyboard will repeat that keystroke until you release that key. This repeating key feature may cause problems for you until you get used to it. It is best to strike most keys with a quick tap.

In computer terminology, a **buffer** is a holding area that can temporarily store computer characters. For example, the keyboard has a buffer that retains keystrokes until the program you are using has "caught up" with you. When you use a program that processes input data slower than it is

Figure 1.5
Summary of Keyboard Keys

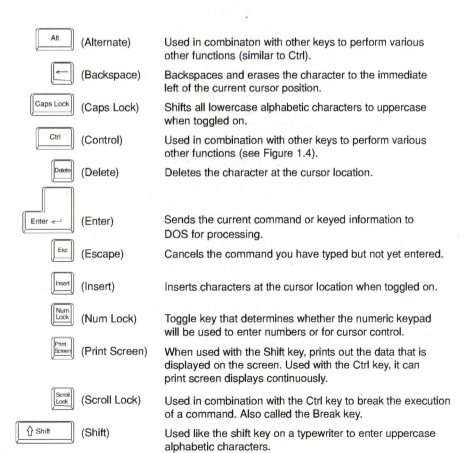

(Alternate)   Used in combinaton with other keys to perform various other functions (similar to Ctrl).

(Backspace)   Backspaces and erases the character to the immediate left of the current cursor position.

(Caps Lock)   Shifts all lowercase alphabetic characters to uppercase when toggled on.

(Control)   Used in combination with other keys to perform various other functions (see Figure 1.4).

(Delete)   Deletes the character at the cursor location.

(Enter)   Sends the current command or keyed information to DOS for processing.

(Escape)   Cancels the command you have typed but not yet entered.

(Insert)   Inserts characters at the cursor location when toggled on.

(Num Lock)   Toggle key that determines whether the numeric keypad will be used to enter numbers or for cursor control.

(Print Screen)   When used with the Shift key, prints out the data that is displayed on the screen. Used with the Ctrl key, it can print screen displays continuously.

(Scroll Lock)   Used in combination with the Ctrl key to break the execution of a command. Also called the Break key.

(Shift)   Used like the shift key on a typewriter to enter uppercase alphabetic characters.

being keyed, the buffer can save keystrokes for processing. If you happen to lay your textbook on the keyboard, pressing keys repeatedly, the buffer will overflow and the computer will begin beeping to alert you to the problem. Buffers are also used to improve the efficiency of processing disk files, which will be discussed in a later chapter.

The Monitor

In addition to requiring the use of a keyboard, personal computers need a **monitor** (screen) to communicate with the user. Keystrokes entered at the keyboard display on the screen to provide visual verification. When the computer communicates with you, it normally displays data, error messages, and system prompts on the screen. Monitors typically display 80 characters on a line and 25 lines on the screen.

Monitors are either monochrome or color. Monochrome monitors are limited to a single color such as amber, green, or white. Most users prefer color monitors to take full advantage of software applications designed to display many different colors.

The sharpness and clarity of images on the screen are directly related to the **screen resolution.** The higher the resolution, the clearer the image becomes on the screen. Screen resolution is usually measured by the number of **picture elements (pixels)** on a screen that can be lit to form images. The lowest resolution monitors display 320 pixels horizontally and 200 pixels vertically (320x200) on the screen. The highest resolution monitors, like those used by engineers and artists for computer graphics, may have 1024x1024 pixels, or more.

Control units, called **video display adapters,** enable the monitor to communicate with the CPU. A Color Graphics Adapter (CGA) monitor is limited to 16 colors in the text mode, or 4 colors in the graphics mode of operation. CGA video display adapters have been replaced with more powerful adapters, such as EGA (Enhanced Graphics Adapter) or VGA (Video Graphics Array) cards. Figure 1.6 shows the major differences among the newer types of monitors. The resolution is directly related to the number of colors displayed on the screen. Monitors are designed to be downward-compatible. Thus, a VGA monitor can run software designed for a CGA or EGA monitor, but not software designed for a Super VGA monitor.

The Printer

Printers for PCs can be classified as either letter quality or draft quality (dot matrix). Most **letter-quality printers** create each character by striking a fully formed image of a character against an inked ribbon and

Figure 1.6
Capabilities of Common Monitors

	EGA		VGA		SUPER VGA	
Number of colors	64	only 16	256	only 16	256	only 16
Resolution (pixels)	320×200	640×350	320×300	640×480	640×480	800×600

paper. They print documents that look as if they were created by a typewriter. **Draft-quality printers** use a dot matrix technique that creates a pattern of dots to represent each character or image. They produce images of lesser quality but are sufficient for most applications. Many dot matrix printers produce near-letter-quality output by reprinting each character, adding dots to fill in the image with a denser pattern of dots. Printing additional dots increases printing time. However, **dot matrix printers** are usually faster and less expensive than letter-quality printers. In addition, dot matrix printers are more flexible in that they can print a wide variety of patterns, including graphics.

Alternatives to inked ribbon printers include ink jet and laser printers. These nonimpact printers are very quiet. **Ink jet printers** spray ink on a page to create high-quality characters. A relatively inexpensive type of ink jet printer, called a bubble jet printer, may be used at home to create letter-quality documents. The fastest and most expensive type of printer is the **laser printer.** It uses a process similar to that of copy machines. Laser printers produce letter-quality output, including graphic images. They allow for many different sizes and styles of characters. They also have the ability to print output sideways, in landscape mode. Laser printers are used extensively in many business and desktop publishing applications.

The Mouse

Most PCs let you use a **mouse** as an input and pointing device. As you move the mouse across a flat surface, it relays information to the computer that moves the cursor (usually shown as an arrow) in the same direction. You press a button on the mouse (similar to pressing the Enter key) to inform the computer that you have selected the desired spot on the screen. Special software, called a mouse driver, is required to use a mouse to control the cursor. This software is normally included when you purchase the mouse hardware.

The Modem

To communicate with other computers via telephone lines, you need at least two items: a modem (at each end) and communications software. A **modem** converts the computer's digital signals to the analog signals used by telephones, and vice versa. A modem at the other end converts an analog tone back to a digital character, such as 01000001. The speed with which the modem can send and receive data is known as its **baud rate**. The higher the baud rate, the less time it takes to send and receive data. Common baud rates are 1200 and 2400, but data can be sent over phone lines at rates as high as 9600 baud. If you divide the baud rate by 10, you can approximate the data transmission rate in characters per second. Thus, 2400 baud is approximately 240 characters per second.

Communications software is readily available to enable you to use your modem effectively. The major purpose of communications software is to guide you through setting up the various communications parameters required to let your computer talk to another computer. Communication parameters include the baud rate, information for encoding/decoding the bit patterns, and methods used for error detection and correction during transmission.

The I/O Interface

Any **input/output (I/O) device** attached to a CPU needs a control unit to allow it to interact with the CPU and make the proper translations between it and the CPU. Each control unit, called an **interface board**, consists of a sturdy card containing electronic chips. These easily removed cards plug directly into slots on the CPU's system board.

The **system board** is the large printed circuit board that contains your microprocessor and primary storage RAM chips. The number of **expansion slots** available depends on the system board. System boards often have expansion slots for a monitor (video display adapter), two serial devices (such as a mouse and a modem), a parallel device (such as a printer), and slots for disk drives. Each slot is connected to a common communications link called a **data bus**. The bigger the data bus, the faster data can be processed inside the CPU. The bus on a PC uses either an 8-, 16-, or 32-bit path.

Slots for a variety of serial and parallel devices are called **ports.** Data is sent through a serial port via a single wire, one bit at a time. Most serial ports use an industry standard called the RS-232 serial interface. Because each character requires eight bits, serial transmission is relatively slow. Faster speeds can obtained with a parallel port. These ports use eight parallel wires to send data eight bits at a time.

Secondary Storage

When you create data on a computer or write programs, nothing is saved permanently in RAM, the computer's primary storage area. RAM is not large enough to store even a modest number of files containing data or programs. **Secondary storage** facilities store large amounts of data on a permanent basis. The cost per bit of secondary storage is far less than that of primary storage. PCs support several types of secondary storage devices, including removable floppy disks and fixed hard disks.

Floppy Disks

Floppy disks are the most common medium for secondary storage and come in various sizes (see Figure 1.7). Initially, the most common size for PCs was the 5 1/4-inch disk, which held 360KB (roughly 360,000 characters) of data. Disk drives record data on circular positions around the surface of the disk, called tracks. A 360KB floppy disk has 40 tracks per side for storing data. High-density 5 1/4-inch disks have a higher quality magnetic coating on the surface of the disk; they can fit 80 tracks on a side, storing 1,200,000 bytes (1.2MB) of data. The most common floppy disk today is the 3 1/2-inch disk. These disks come in a hard

Figure 1.7
Floppy Disks

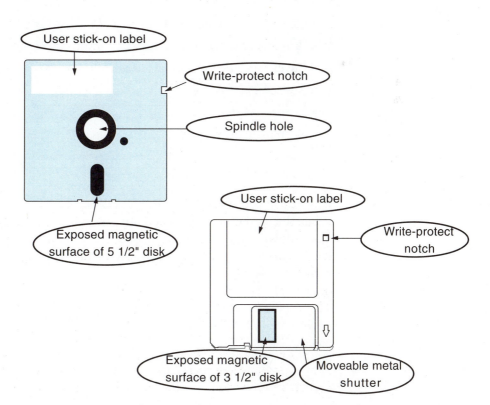

plastic case and use improved technology to record data as follows: 720KB (low density), 1.44MB (high density), or 2.88MB (ultra-high density) of data.

When you insert a 5 1/4-inch floppy disk into a floppy disk drive and close the latch, the disk is secured by two clamps that close on the large center hole of the disk. If the latch is not securely closed, an error message will inform you that the disk cannot be accessed. When data is read from or written to a 5 1/4-inch disk, a motor connected to the clamps spins the disk inside its protective jacket. A small red light on the disk drive indicates the drive is spinning. *Do not remove the disk when the red light is on.*

Floppy disks are not completely reliable because they can be easily damaged. However, if you take proper precautions, floppy disks can serve you faithfully for a long time. Figure 1.8 contains some helpful and important tips for using floppy disks.

Figure 1.8

Proper Care of Floppy Disks

- Always store floppies in their protective covers when not in use.
- Store them vertically to lessen the chances of warping.
- Shade them from direct sunlight and intense heat.
- Write on any attached labels with felt-tip pens only.
- Never touch the recording surface of a floppy disk.
- Never bend, fold, or otherwise crimp a floppy disk.
- Keep disks free of contaminants, including smoke.
- Keep them away from magnetic sources, such as electric motors.

Hard disks are also called fixed disks because they are not removable. When the hard disk drive is operating, it spins much faster than a floppy disk, allowing for greater access speeds. In addition, you do not have to continually swap disks. Hard disks typically hold 40MB, 80MB, or even hundreds of megabytes of data. Hard disks store data using a much higher density, allowing for many more tracks per side than floppy disks. This is because the disk surfaces are rigid metal platters in a sealed environment, free from contamination. A 40MB hard disk, for example, can store more data than 100 360KB floppy disks. Figure 1.9 shows a hard disk with a cut-away view of the platter.

Figure 1.9
Hard Disk

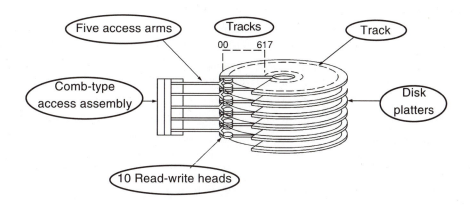

It is not practical for personal computers to have only a hard disk drive. Floppy disks are used for transferring data and programs from one computer to another and for backup. Applications generally require at least one hard disk drive and one floppy disk drive. Figure 1.10 identifies the major differences between these two types of disks.

Figure 1.10
Comparison of Floppy Disks and Hard Disks

	FLOPPY DISK	HARD DISK
Portability	Removable	Fixed
Processing Speed	Very slow	Much faster
Storage Capacity	Relatively small	Very large
Reliability	Easily damaged	More secure

In addition to hardware, a computer system must have **software** to control and operate the hardware. Figure 1.11 outlines the various classifications of software.

Figure 1.11
PC Software

```
                    ┌── Application Software
Software ───────────┤
                    │                       ┌── Operating system (DOS)
                    └── System Software ─────┤
                                            └── Utility Support Programs
```

Application Software

Application software is a set of programmed instructions written for a specific purpose, such as word processing or inventory. A large number of prewritten programs are available at a reasonable cost. An abundance of application software has been written for PCs, including the following general categories:

- *Word processing programs* that let you create and modify documents.
- *Electronic spreadsheet programs* to manipulate numeric data.
- *Database programs* for keeping track of things, such as customers.
- *Communications programs* that let you "talk" to other computers.
- *Spreadsheet programs* for accounting, budgeting, payroll, and so on.

System Software

Your computer system needs an **operating system** to act as a translator between the application programs and the hardware. Application programs can run on a computer only after the operating system has been loaded. This process, called "booting the system," is covered later. The operating system lets you control the computer's operations and manage files. Most operating systems let you use the computer in either an interactive or a batch mode. With **interactive processing**, the user enters a command for the computer to execute immediately. When the computer finishes that command, the user issues another command. **Batch processing** occurs after a user creates and saves a file of commands. Once the batch file is created, the user can enter a single command that tells the system to execute all the commands in the file one after another. This text covers both methods of processing.

System software normally includes an operating system and a set of supporting utility programs. For example, the operating system we will be discussing is DOS (Disk Operating System). It is normally included when you purchase a PC. Even with its power and many capabilities, many users found the need for additional software. To make DOS easier to use, they turned to **utility support programs,** such as Automenu or Treeview. Other utility programs, such as Microsoft Windows, Norton Utilities, and PC-Tools, provide additional capabilities not found in DOS. Appendix B discusses utility support programs and provides many more examples.

The last topic to discuss before delving into DOS is a hybrid type of hardware, called **ROM (Read-Only Memory)**, which is used to store preprogrammed instructions. Special-purpose programs are built into ROM chips during manufacturing. Because ROM programs are permanently embedded into computer memory, they can be executed without having to be loaded into RAM. ROM is a form of nonvolatile (permanent) memory. Unlike RAM, it does not lose its instructions when the power is turned off. Therefore, ROM is often used to hold operating system startup programs and language translators, such as BASIC. If you have an IBM-PC (not an IBM clone or compatible), the instructions for interpreting BASIC programs are contained on a proprietary ROM chip.

When you turn on your computer system, a ROM chip first tests the hardware for problems. Then it loads a portion of DOS from the default disk drive. In the future, more software (including DOS) will be available in the form of inexpensive ROM chips. Laptops and other portable PCs may contain both the operating system and several common application programs in ROM. This will make them lighter and faster, and reduce the amount of disk storage required.

Chapter 1

Review Questions

1. What are the four major hardware parts of a PC?
2. What is the major difference between primary storage and secondary storage?
3. What is the major difference between RAM and ROM?
4. What is the purpose of a clock rate in a microprocessor?
5. What is the potential danger of static electricity?
6. What is the purpose of function keys?
7. What is a toggle key?
8. Give two examples of toggle keys found on the keyboard.
9. Give two examples of combination keys found on the keyboard.
10. What happens when you press the Backspace key?
11. Describe the repeating key concept.
12. What term defines the sharpness and clarity of images on the display screen?
13. What is the significance of having more bits in an addressable unit of RAM?
14. What are some advantages that dot matrix printers have over letter-quality printers?
15. What are the two most common forms of secondary storage on PCs?

16. What are the major differences between hard disks and floppy disks?

17. What is the difference between application and system software?

18. What are the major benefits of utility support programs?

19. What is the difference between batch and interactive processing?

20. What is the function of a data bus?

Chapter 1

Exercises

1. Using what you learned in this chapter, make a list of the components for the computers in your lab. This may require asking some questions because not all of the information may be obvious.

2. Match the seven components (labeled A-G) in Figure 1.12 to the component names provided below. As in the previous exercise, this may require some additional information. However, you should be able to make some good "educated guesses" from the material covered in this chapter.

Figure 1.12
Personal Computer and Data Bus

Microprocessor

Data Bus

Data Bus Controller

A

B   C   D   E   F   G

Primary Storage Keyboard Monitor Disk Drive Printer Mouse

___ Parallel port   ___ Random Access Memory

___ Serial port   ___ Keyboard interface

___ Internal clock   ___ Disk controller

___ Display adapter

3. Using information obtained from computer magazines, newspapers, or people who sell PCs, find the current price range for each of the following hardware items:

	Without Controller	With Controller
Super VGA Monitor	_____	_____
LaserJet Printer	_____	N/A
Mouse (with software)	_____	N/A
Internal Modem	_____	N/A
Floppy Disk Drive (3 1/2")	_____	_____
Hard Disk (120MB)	_____	_____

INTRODUCTION TO DOS CONCEPTS

BASIC DOS FUNCTIONS

> **Control Input/Output Operations**
>
> **Interpret and Execute Commands**
>
> **Manage Files**

SAVING FILES WITH DOS

WORKING WITH HARD DISKS

UNDERSTANDING DIRECTORIES AND SUBDIRECTORIES

BOOTING DOS

> **Booting from a Floppy Disk**
>
> **Entering the Date and Time**
>
> **Booting from a Hard Disk**

INTRODUCTION TO DOS CONCEPTS

The primary goal of Chapter 2 is to teach you the basic functions of DOS for command processing and file management. By the end of this chapter, you will understand how files are saved on disk, why we use subdirectories with hard disks, and how to load (boot) DOS.

An **operating system,** such as DOS, is a set of programs that is an integral part of all computer systems. Without an operating system, you would not be able to use your computer. For example, suppose you wanted to use your computer to create a term paper with a word processing program. The operating system allows you to load and execute programs. In addition, application programs use the operating system to save and retrieve disk files. Your computer's operating system provides all this capability, and more.

The operating system is a necessary translator between the hardware and application programs. The operating system coordinates and controls all activities of the computer (see Figure 2.1). It also contains a group of commands and programs that lets you interact directly with the computer. For example, it provides an easy way to copy data from one disk to another, allowing you to make backup copies of important data. Having an understanding of DOS will help you run your application programs and will make you a more effective user.

Figure 2.1
The Role of an Operating System

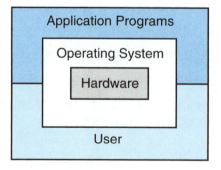

This chapter introduces you to a specific type of disk operating system (DOS) called IBM DOS or MS-DOS. Both operating systems are used with IBM and IBM-compatible PCs. Some users are confused by the terms IBM DOS and MS-DOS, as the two operating systems are very similar. IBM DOS is IBM's implementation of DOS 5. MS-DOS is Microsoft's version and can be used on all IBM-compatible PCs. IBM and Microsoft have worked closely together to keep both implementations of DOS nearly identical. Because of the similarities of IBM DOS and MS-DOS, this text refers to either operating system simply as DOS. Whenever they differ, the specific operating system is identified.

BASIC DOS FUNCTIONS

DOS has three major functions to help you use your computer. It controls the input and output operations of your computer, it interprets and executes commands entered from your keyboard, and it saves files on disk and lets you manage them effectively.

Control Input/ Output Operations

All application programs share the same input and output problems. They all accept data from the keyboard, display data on the monitor, store data temporarily in main memory, store data permanently on disk, and retrieve data from disks. It requires many instructions to coordinate and control activities on a PC. Without an operating system, each application program would have to duplicate these instructions.

On a MS-DOS disk there are two "hidden files," **MSDOS.SYS** and **IO.SYS**. These hidden system files provide the input/output instructions required by DOS and by application programs. **Hidden files** do not appear on your screen when you list the files on your DOS disk. MSDOS.SYS provides all the support functions necessary for application programs to run on your system. These functions are primarily related to disk operations. IO.SYS contains additions to the basic I/O system routines built into your system on ROM chips. IO.SYS holds the device drivers (instructions) DOS uses to operate other devices attached to your system, such as the screen, printer, and keyboard. In IBM DOS, these two hidden files are named **IBMDOS.COM** and **IBMBIO.COM.**

Interpret and Execute Commands

The command processor part of DOS interprets and executes the commands you enter, as well as commands from application programs. Without an operating system, you would have no effective way to communicate with the hardware and direct its activities. In MS-DOS and IBM DOS these functions are in the **COMMAND.COM** file.

Manage Files

As a user, you are heavily involved with the file management role of DOS. For example, before you can save files you must prepare (format) the disk to record files. Once a disk is formatted you may save, rename, copy, or delete files. DOS provides a series of commands to allow users and application programs to manage the multitude of disk files created over time. Most of this text is devoted to file management commands.

SAVING FILES WITH DOS

A **file** is a set of related information items saved as a single group and given a filename. Because the information saved consists of either program instructions or data, a file is either an executable **program file** or a **data file.** For example, a word processing program is a program file and a document you create with it is a data file. When you save a file with a filename that already exists on the disk, the contents of the existing file are deleted and replaced by the information in the new file. If you save a file with a new name, it is automatically added to the disk.

Saving files on disk is a function of all operating systems. The files you create and work with in RAM are temporary and become permanent only when you save them on disk. When you turn off the computer or otherwise lose power, the contents of RAM (program and data files) are erased. However, files saved on disk can be recalled when needed. Application programs routinely direct DOS to save files. Although it may seem like a simple process, many steps are required to save files. The following overview explains this process.

(1) IBM and IBM-compatible floppy disk drives are double-sided, meaning data is stored on both sides of the disk. Disk speed is increased when you access both sides of a disk before moving to another track. The areas on a formatted disk used to record data are made up of **sectors** and **tracks** (see Figure 2.2). Identical sectors on the top and bottom surface of a disk are combined to form a cluster. A **cluster** is the smallest addressable location that can save data on a disk. In DOS 5, the term

Figure 2.2

Partial Diagram of a Floppy Disk

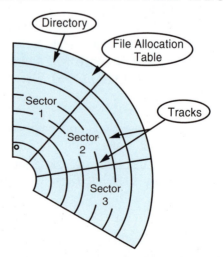

allocation unit also refers to a cluster. Each sector on a 360KB disk contains 512 bytes, so the cluster size is 1024 bytes. The size of the cluster varies depending on the disk drive used and the number of read/ write heads per track. Large cluster sizes improve performance of disk access when files are large. When files are smaller than a cluster, the unused space in the cluster cannot be used by another file.

(2) When you issue a save command from an application program or directly from DOS, the operating system finds an unused area (unallocated clusters) to store the file. Because DOS uses whatever clusters it can find to store the file, the clusters are not always adjoining. Files written in noncontiguous (non-adjoining) clusters are called **fragmented files.** The additional head movement caused by fragmentation slows down the time it takes to process these files. Figure 2.3 shows how file fragmentation occurs.

Figure 2.3
File Fragmentation

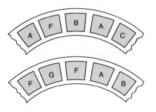

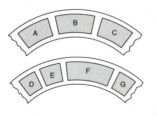

1. As you create files on a brand new disk, they are stored on the disk one after another such as File A, File B, and so on. Each file occupies contiguous clusters on the disk and disk performance is at its peak.

2. Whenever you delete a file, a "hole" is left where the file was stored. As you save more files, DOS may fill that hole with parts of other files, causing file fragmentation. Over time, pieces of your files can be scattered all over your disk.The time required to access fragmented files can be many times slower than nonfragmented files, depending on the extent of fragmentation.

3. One way to eliminate fragmentation of files is to copy all your files to a newly formatted disk. Or, you can purchase a disk optimization program to rearrange your files into contiguous clusters on the same disk. A disk optimizer is highly recommended for hard disk systems.

(3) DOS keeps track of which clusters are used and which ones are free to store data. This area of the disk is called the **File Allocation Table (FAT).** When DOS saves a file, the FAT is updated with the cluster information used to store (and retrieve) the file.

(4) DOS then updates the **directory** on the disk with important information about the file. The directory, along with the FAT, is stored in a reserved area of track zero on each disk. The file information stored on the disk's directory is as follows:

- filename and filename extension
- file size (in bytes)
- date and time of creation or last update
- starting cluster location in the FAT
- status of file attributes

Each file has four specific qualities called **attributes.** The status of each attribute is stored as file information on the disk directory as follows:

- The **archive** attribute is used by BACKUP, XCOPY, and other DOS commands to determine whether or not files have been saved (archived) to another location. When files are created (or subsequently modified), DOS sets the archive attribute on, indicating that it has not been saved.
- The **read-only** attribute is used to protect a file from being accidentally changed or deleted. When the read-only attribute is set on (with the ATTRIB command), you may read the file, but you cannot change or delete it without first setting the attribute off.
- The **hidden** attribute tells DOS to bypass displaying the filename on a normal directory listing.
- The **system** attribute identifies a DOS system file. These files contain data relating to your hardware and system software.

WORKING WITH HARD DISKS

As noted in Chapter 1, hard disks have two significant advantages over floppy disks: the speed at which data is transferred is significantly faster, and the amount of data that can be stored per disk is much greater. The following operational items relate to hard disk systems.

1. The first consideration is the need for a *good power supply* that does not permit loss of electrical power. A temporary power loss may cause the disk's read/write heads to "crash" on the surface of the disk, causing permanent damage. To ensure continuous power for hard disk systems, a standby power supply is recommended. A continuous supply of electricity protects data stored on the disk as well as the disk drive. For a cost of about $300, buying a good power backup system for business computers is a good investment.

2. Another consideration is the need for *periodic backup* of the data stored on your hard disk. Backup means to copy important files to floppy disks. Although backup is equally important for data stored on floppy disks, hard disk users often overlook this important operation. Get into the habit of backing up your hard disk regularly. You will be glad you did the day you turn on your computer and hear a noise like a spoon in a blender.

3. The last consideration is the need to *"park" (move) the read/write* heads to an unused area of the hard disk before you "power down" the system. When the power is turned off, the read/write heads on older hard disk drives do not retract automatically. Instead, the heads remain over the recording surface. If the computer is moved and the heads are not secured, the disk can become damaged. Most hard disks purchased today automatically retract and secure the heads. If you are not sure what kind of disk drive you have, run a program to park the heads just prior to turning off the power. Utility programs, like BYE, PARK, and SHIP, move the heads to a vacant track and secure them for shipping. If a parking program came with your system, be sure to use it!

UNDERSTANDING DIRECTORIES AND SUBDIRECTORIES

Because large amounts of data are stored on a hard disk, users find it necessary to divide the total space into uniquely named areas. Each area, called a **subdirectory,** is used to store a specific group of files. Subdirectories let you organize and classify files by application. You can establish subdirectories on floppy disks, but using directories is essential with hard disks. Hard disks have too many files to keep track of without organizing them into logical subdirectories. The term *directory* is often used to represent a subdirectory. Therefore, we will use the term *directory* interchangeably.

One way to visualize the concept of directories is to compare a single 40MB hard disk to a set of 110 floppy disks. Conceptually, each directory can represent a single floppy disk, without the physical size limitations. Like floppy disks, each directory can be devoted to a given application, such as word processing, spreadsheet, accounting, and so on. You can change to a specific directory, just as you insert another floppy disk.

Another way to think of directories is to relate them to how data is organized in a filing cabinet. Each drawer in a cabinet could be thought of as a directory. The large hanging folders in each drawer could represent dozens of lower-level directories, within each of the main directories. Additionally, the individual file folders in the hanging folders could be even lower-level directories.

You can organize and control hundreds of files on a hard disk by adopting a tree-structured file directory system. The **root directory** branches into directories. Each directory can branch into further directories. The tree-like hierarchy is similar to a family tree or business organization chart. Figure 2.4 shows an example of a tree-structured directory on a hard disk.

Figure 2.4

Sample Hierarchy of Directories

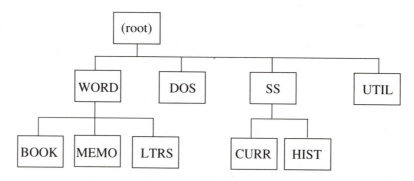

In this typical tree structure, the root directory is divided into four directories: one for word processing, one for DOS, one for spreadsheets, and one for utility programs. The word processing directory (WORD) is further divided into three directories: manuscripts, memos, and letters. DOS navigates through this structure by starting at the root and traveling down any of the desired branches to get to the desired directory.

Floppy disk files are often organized manually by saving selected groups of files on a disk and identifying each disk with a sticky label. Hard disk directories provide a big advantage in that they allow you to organize all the files "electronically." Files may be added quickly and new directories may be created as needed.

BOOTING DOS

Before any computer can be used, its operating system must be loaded into RAM. There is not enough room in RAM to store all of DOS, so only a small portion of DOS is loaded at a time. Loading is known as **booting the system.**

There are two ways to boot DOS. One way is called a **cold boot** — the computer is off prior to the boot process and the hardware is cold. A **warm boot** is used when the computer is already on, but needs to be booted again.

The major difference between the two ways of booting the system is how the boot process begins. For a cold boot, you turn on the computer to boot DOS. For a warm boot, you enter a sequence of three keys simultaneously: the Control key, the Alternate key, and the Delete key **(Ctrl-Alt-Del).** Most newer PCs have a reset button that can be pressed to do a warm boot.

Because the computer is an electronic device, do a warm boot whenever possible. The sudden surge of electricity that occurs when the power is turned on can sometimes damage sensitive electronic chips. There is one good reason for a cold boot, however, when sharing a computer with others. A cold boot erases RAM, helping to prevent the spread of virus programs from previous users.

Booting from a Floppy Disk

To do a cold boot of DOS from a floppy disk, insert the disk containing DOS in Drive A. Drive A is usually the top or leftmost drive in PCs with two floppy disk drives. To initiate the cold boot, turn on the power to both the monitor and the CPU. The boot process involves the six steps shown in Figure 2.5 and described below.

(1) The PC begins by executing a small startup program stored in a ROM chip to run some predetermined diagnostic tests. These tests include checking the computer's RAM and keyboard to make sure they are functional. If there are any problems, the program displays an error message on your screen. For example, if your computer beeps and displays "KEYBOARD ERROR PRESS F1 TO RE-SUME," your keyboard may be disconnected. If this happens, turn off the system, plug in the keyboard, and do another cold boot.

(2) After the computer passes the diagnostic checks, the program in ROM loads the two hidden DOS files from your DOS disk in Drive A. These hidden files remain in RAM as long as the power stays on.

(3) At this point, DOS looks for an optional **CONFIG.SYS** file used to specify some of the different ways your system can be configured, or customized. The CONFIG.SYS file is covered in Chapter 10.

Figure 2.5
The Boot Process

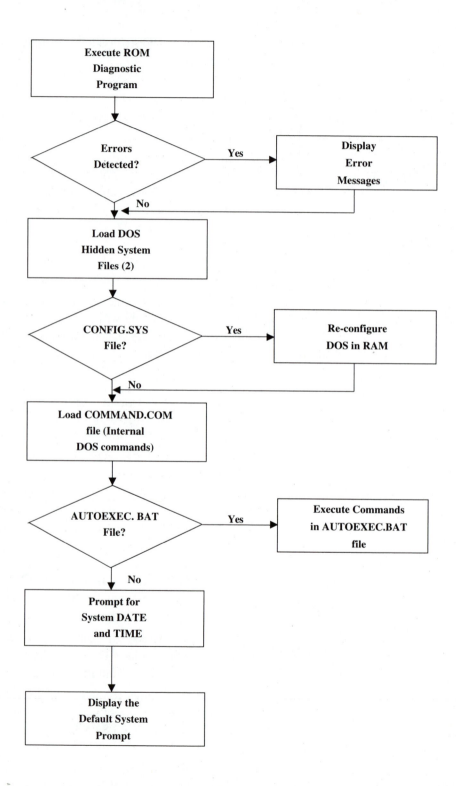

(4) Then, DOS loads a file called COMMAND.COM into RAM from Drive A. **COMMAND.COM** contains many of the commands you will use, including instructions to load and process all commands entered.

(5) DOS looks for another file on Drive A called **AUTOEXEC.BAT**. If found, DOS executes any additional instructions it contains. Using an AUTOEXEC.BAT file, explained in Chapter 9, can simplify the booting process by executing the same set of commands each time you boot the system.

(6) If there is no AUTOEXEC.BAT file, DOS waits for you to enter the correct date and time. DOS has its own system clock to keep track of the time while the computer is on. After obtaining the date and time, DOS displays the version number of the operating system and prompts you to enter a command.

Entering the Date and Time

The system date is entered using month, day, and year in the form of mm-dd-yy. You can use either a slash (/), a hyphen (-), or a period (.) to separate the date entries. As with all operating systems, when you a enter a command or some data, like the date or time, you must press the Enter key to let the system know you are finished keying. Figure 2.6 shows you how the screen might look after you entered a

Figure 2.6
Screen Display after Booting DOS 5

```
Current date is Fri 07-03-1993
Enter new date (mm-dd-yy): 7-4-93
Current time is 3:33:07.69p
Enter new time: 1:45p
Microsoft(R) MS-DOS(R) Version 5.00 (C)Copyright
Microsoft Corp 1981-1991.

A> _
```

date of July 4, 1993 and a time of 1:45 p.m. For illustrative purposes, the data entered is shown in boldface.

Enter the system time using hours, minutes, seconds, and hundredths of seconds in the form of hh:mm:ss:xx. The use of minutes (mm), seconds (ss), and hundredths of seconds (xx) is optional. You may enter time using the 24-hour system (military time) or the 12-hour system. To use the 12-hour system, key in the appropriate letter (a or p) after the time. Use the colon (:) or a period (.) to separate time entries. Thus, you may enter **13.45, 13:45, 1.45p,** or **1:45p** to indicate 1:45 in the afternoon.

After DOS is booted, you are prompted to enter a command. When booting from a floppy disk, the initial system prompt is A>, where A is the disk drive containing DOS. The underline character following the system prompt is the cursor. Your next keystroke will be placed (echoed) on the screen at the cursor location.

To change the date after DOS is booted, enter **DATE** (or **date**) at the system prompt and press the Enter key. Any combination of uppercase and lowercase letters can be used to enter DOS commands. DOS displays the current date for you and asks you for a new date. The format of the new date is the same as with the boot process (mm-dd-yy). When entering the date, you do not have to enter leading zeros. For example, enter **07** or **7** for July. You do not have to enter the century. Thus, you can enter **93** to represent 1993.

To change the time, enter **TIME** (or **time**) and press Enter. Change the time using the same syntax as before. For example, you can enter **20:15** or **8:15p** to represent 8:15 p.m. DATE and TIME are two DOS commands covered in Chapter 5.

Booting from a Hard Disk

The boot process is almost identical for hard disk systems with two exceptions:

(**1**) If there is no floppy disk in Drive A, most PC systems are designed to look for the files needed to boot the system on the hard disk, which is Drive C. When booting from a hard disk, be certain there is no floppy disk in Drive A and that Drive A is unlatched. Whenever Drive C is used to boot the system, C> (or something similar) becomes the initial system prompt.

(**2**) Most hard disk systems have a battery-operated clock-calendar that keeps track of the date and time when the power is off. Typically, a program in ROM contains instructions that automatically sets the system clock (date and time) from this battery-operated clock.

Chapter 2

Review Questions

1. What are the main purposes of an operating system?
2. What does "booting the system" mean?
3. Why are there hidden files on a DOS disk?
4. Why do you think DOS writes on both sides of a floppy disk before moving to another track?
5. Why should you boot your system with the correct date and time?
6. What is the function of the File Allocation Table (FAT)?
7. What is the difference between a warm boot and a cold boot?
8. How do you tell DOS to do a warm boot?
9. What is the purpose of the COMMAND.COM file?
10. When are commands in an AUTOEXEC.BAT file executed?
11. How can you change the system date after the system is booted?
12. How would you enter a time of 2:35 p.m. when prompted to do so?
13. What is the difference between MS-DOS and IBM DOS?
14. What is the difference between a program file and a data file?
15. Describe a cluster, or allocation unit.
16. How do disk files become fragmented?
17. What is the purpose of a disk's directory?
18. What is a file attribute?
19. How can you protect a disk file from being accidentally deleted?
20. Describe a directory.

Chapter 2

Floppy Disk Lab Exercise

This exercise assumes that the system is already turned on. If it is not on, do a cold boot before you continue. This exercise is for computers with two floppy disk drives. The DOS disk should be in Drive A. If you are working with a hard disk system with a single floppy disk, skip ahead to the hard disk exercise.

Perform a warm boot from a floppy disk:

1. With the DOS disk in Drive A, use Ctrl-Alt-Del to boot the system.
2. Enter the date in mm-dd-yy format (for example, 9-15-93).
3. Enter the time in hh:mm format (for example, 13:07 or 1.07p).
4. Press the Enter key to cause the computer to act on your data.

This completes the Chapter 2 floppy disk lab exercise. Please remove your DOS disk before you leave the computer.

Chapter 2

Hard Disk Lab Exercise

The DOS commands should already be loaded on your hard disk (C:). They should be stored in a separate and specific directory on the hard disk. If your computer is off, do a cold boot before proceeding.

Perform a warm boot from a hard disk:

1. Remove any floppy disk from Drive A and press Ctrl-Alt-Del to warm boot the system.

2. If your computer does not have a battery-operated clock that auto-matically sets the system clock when you boot the system, you will have to enter the date in mm-dd-yy format (i.e., 9-15-93). Then, enter the time in hh:mm format (i.e., 8:07 or 2:15p). Don't forget to press the Enter key to cause the computer to act on your data.

This completes the Chapter 2 hard disk lab exercise.

INTRODUCTION TO DOS COMMANDS

INTRODUCTION TO DOS COMMANDS

The objective of Chapter 3 is to provide a general understanding of DOS commands. Because DOS is consistent in applying these fundamental concepts, it is easier to learn how use DOS commands once you understand these basic concepts. This chapter will to introduce you to the syntax used to enter DOS commands, using the HELP and FORMAT commands as examples. The HELP command lets you obtain on-line help concerning the use and syntax of any DOS command. The FORMAT command is needed to prepare disks for recording data.

FUNDAMENTAL DOS COMMAND CONCEPTS

Before learning specific DOS commands, it is helpful to understand the basic concepts applicable to all DOS commands. The concepts include:

- The default disk drive
- Standard device names used by DOS
- The need for effective file naming conventions
- DOS directory listings
- The use of wildcard characters
- Internal and external DOS commands
- Versions of DOS

Default Disk Drive

Most computer systems have at least two disk drives. Applications on floppy disk systems often require that a program disk be located in one drive and your data disk in another. If your computer has only one floppy disk, it will likely also have a hard disk. A hard disk can easily store both application programs and data. However, you still need a floppy disk drive to load files from floppy disks to the hard disk or to make backup copies of your hard disk files.

When running DOS, the system needs to know what disk drive is the target of the commands you enter. DOS employs the **default drive** concept, referred to often in this book. DOS lets you specify which of the disk drives is to be the default. Whenever you enter a command and do not specify a disk drive, DOS substitutes the default drive for the missing one(s) in the command. By understanding how DOS uses the default drive concept, you can save keystrokes when entering commands. *Remember, you only need to designate a disk drive if it is other than the* *default drive.* In the beginning, however, it is best if you learn to enter the disk drive to help you understand how DOS operates.

To identify the different disk drives, DOS uses a coding scheme consisting of letters: A and B are used for floppy drives; C through Z are used for hard disk drives. The drive used to boot the system is the initial default disk. You can change the default to become another drive at any time. If you booted DOS from a floppy disk and got the A> prompt, the A refers to the default disk drive. If you booted from a hard disk, the default disk is Drive C. The > is the symbol used by DOS to help identify the system prompt. This is the way DOS reminds you which drive is the current default drive.

To change the default drive, you must enter a new disk drive letter followed by a colon. For example, to change the default drive from A to B, type B: and press the Enter key as follows:

FLOPPY DISK SYSTEM	**HARD DISK SYSTEM**
`A> B: <Enter>`	`C> A: <Enter>`

Once entered, DOS logs onto the new drive, the default drive is changed, and a new system prompt is displayed. Because DOS reads the new disk, you will get an error message if the new drive does not contain a formatted disk. To change the default disk back enter:

FLOPPY DISK SYSTEM	**HARD DISK SYSTEM**
`B> A: <Enter>`	`A> C: <Enter>`

Standard Device Names

DOS reserves certain names to represent system devices. For example, the reserved word **PRN** refers to the printer. Printer designations can be used to copy a file to your printer for a hard copy listing. Because reserved words have specific meanings to DOS, you should never use them to name a file. Figure 3.1 contains a listing of some of these device names.

Figure 3.1
Reserved DOS
Device Names

DEVICE NAME	DESCRIPTION
AUX	Auxiliary serial port
CLOCK$	System clock
COM*n*	Serial communications port (*n* = 1 to 4)
CON	Console (keyboard)
LPT*n*	Parallel printer port (*n* = 1 to 3)
PRN	Printer (attached to LPT1)

File Naming Conventions

DOS uses the **full filename** to tell it where to search for a file. The full filename consists of four parts: disk drive designator, path, filename, and filename extension. The optional parts are shown in brackets as follows:

```
[d:][path]filename[.ext]
```

The first part of the full filename, **[d:]**, specifies the disk drive. To specify a drive, enter the drive letter followed by a colon. If you omit the drive, the default disk drive is used by DOS.

The next part, **[path]**, is the location of the subdirectory containing the file. For example, all the DOS commands are probably stored in a single subdirectory on a hard disk. If you omit the path, DOS will default to the current subdirectory. A path is not usually required to identify floppy disk files. Floppy disks are rarely divided into subdirectories because of their relatively small size.

Only the **filename** is always required when naming a file. Filenames can be from one to eight characters in length. Filenames can be made up of alphabetic letters, numeric digits, and a few special characters such as hyphens and underscores. You should avoid using any of the special characters, except for the hyphen (-), used to make filenames more readable. Spaces and punctuation such as periods, commas, colons, or semicolons are invalid characters in a filename.

Always use meaningful filenames to further classify the type of data contained in each file. A great deal of information can be coded into your filenames. For example, a set of documents on the new bottling plant could be named BOTTLE1.DOC, BOTTLE2.DOC, and so on. If the memo dates were critical, the filenames could be BOTmmdd.DOC, where mm represents the month created and dd is the day. Later you will see how wildcard characters can be used to select a specific group of files. When you display a sorted file directory, the memos are listed together in chronological sequence. As the number of files grows, the benefits of care and foresight in creating filenames become more significant.

The final part of the full filename is an optional extension. The **extension** uses the same set of characters valid for filenames, but it is limited to three characters. Filename extensions, such as DOC, must be preceded by a period (.DOC). Filename extensions help you to identify the category of each file. When an extension is used within a filename, it becomes a permanent part of the full name. Except for executable program files (see Figure 3.2), the extension must be included when requesting DOS to access the file. You should abide by the standard extensions already established and commonly used. Application programs, which also assign filenames, often use the standard extensions shown in Figure 3.2.

Figure 3.2
Standard Filename
Extensions

Executable files (executed by entering just the filename with no extension):

BAT — Batch file (file containing executable commands)
COM— Machine language program file (limited in size to 64KB)
EXE — Machine language program file (larger than COM files)

Text files (not executable, but can be displayed on the screen):

BAK — Backup text file
BAS — BASIC program file (needs compiling first)
DAT — Data file
DBF — dBASE file
DOC — Documentation file
HLP — Help file (contains help instructions)
INI — Initialization file (like DOSSHELL.INI)
PRN — Printer file (can be modified prior to printing)
SYS — System ASCII file (like CONFIG.SYS)
TXT — Text file

Other files (not executable and not in a form that can be displayed):

DEF — Program definition (setup) file
FON — Font file
GIF — GIF graphics image file
OVL — Overlay file (used by large programs)
PIF — Program information file (memory allocation in Windows)
SYS — System binary file (like ANSI.SYS)
TIF — TIFF graphics image file
WK1 — Lotus 1-2-3 worksheet file
WPG— WordPerfect graphics file

DOS Directory Listings

When DOS displays a **directory listing** on your screen, DOS provides more than just the filenames. The file size in bytes and the date stamp are also displayed for each file listed. The **date stamp** is the date and time that each file was last written to the disk. To assist you in managing files on your disk, you should enter the correct date and time each time DOS is booted. Figure 3.3 shows you a partial directory listing of a DOS 5 disk. The filename extensions are displayed in columnar form to make them easy to find. The <DIR> entries are explained in Chapter 7.

Wildcard Characters

Wildcard characters can be used to represent different filename characters in DOS commands, like jokers in a card game. DOS uses two wildcard characters: the asterisk (*), representing a group of one or more characters, and the question mark (?), representing only a single character.

The best way to understand how wildcard characters are used is by example. The **DIR** command (covered in Chapter 5) can be used to display the names of files stored on a disk. The DIR command can be used with wildcard characters to selectively display a group of filenames. Thus, to display a directory listing of all the files on Drive A that begin with the characters LTR and that have an extension of DOC, you can

Figure 3.3
Partial MS-DOS Disk Directory

```
 Volume in drive C is PENWORTH
 Volume Serial Number is 16F1-A1C6
 Directory of C:\DOS

.            <DIR>        01-01-80   10:57p
..           <DIR>        01-01-80   10:57p
ANSI     SYS      9029 04-09-91    5:00a
APPEND   EXE     10774 04-09-91    5:00a
QBASIC   INI       175 03-28-92    6:29p
ASSIGN   COM      6399 04-09-91    5:00a
ATTRIB   EXE     15796 04-09-91    5:00a
BACKUP   EXE     36092 04-09-91    5:00a
CHKDSK   EXE     16200 04-09-91    5:00a
COMMAND  COM     47845 04-09-91    5:00a
COMP     EXE     14282 04-09-91    5:00a
AUTO     BAT        85 04-17-92    1:41p
COUNTRY  SYS     17069 04-09-91    5:00a
DEBUG    EXE     20634 04-09-91    5:00a
DELOLDOS EXE     17644 04-09-91    5:00a
DISKCOMP COM     10652 04-09-91    5:00a
DISKCOPY COM     11793 04-09-91    5:00a
DISPLAY  SYS     15792 04-09-91    5:00a
DOSHELP  HLP      5651 04-09-91    5:00a
Press any key to continue . . .
```

enter **DIR A:LTR*.DOC**. In this example, the asterisk represents any group of characters, so that files named LTRSMITH.DOC, LTR4.DOC, and LTRBILL3.DOC would be included on the directory listing.

To identify all the files on Drive A that have a single character following LTR, enter **DIR A:LTR?.DOC.** In this example, the filenames LTR1.DOC, LTR2.DOC, and LTRX.DOC would be included. Wildcard characters may also be used with filename extensions as follows:

DIR A:TEXT.*   (list all files on Drive A with a filename of TEXT and having any extension)

DIR A:LTR*.*   (list any filename on Drive A starting with LTR and having an extension)

Try some examples using your DOS disk. If DOS is currently booted, enter the following commands at the system prompt, pressing the Enter key after each command:

DIR   (lists all files on the default disk or directory)

DIR *.EXE   (lists only files with an EXE extension)

DIR S*.*   (lists only files that begin with an S)

DOS automatically translates all command keystrokes to uppercase characters, so you may enter DOS commands using either uppercase or lowercase letters. Furthermore, you can use a combination of both cases. Thus, the commands **Dir, dir,** and **DIR** are treated the same by DOS. To help you remember this feature, many examples in this book use both uppercase and lowercase characters.

Internal and External DOS Commands

A DOS command must be copied into RAM from disk before it can be executed. There is not enough room for all DOS commands to be in RAM at the same time. Therefore, commands are either internal or external commands. **Internal commands** are frequently used DOS commands loaded into RAM when the system is booted. The DIR command is an example of an internal command.

Because there is not enough room in RAM for all of DOS, **external commands** reside on the DOS disk. External commands must be copied into RAM each time they are executed from a floppy disk or a hard disk. Most of the filenames shown in Figure 3.3 with EXE or COM extensions are external DOS commands. The remainder of the files are primarily system files used by DOS.

Versions of DOS   Major releases of DOS often accompany a major improvement in hardware design. The first version of DOS (Version 1) appeared in 1981 along with the IBM PC. It was severely limited and is now obsolete. DOS 2 included hard disk capability, a necessity for business applications. DOS 3 added networking capability, better file management commands, and support for 3 1/2-inch disks. DOS 4 provided a DOS shell, support for hard disks exceeding 32 megabytes, and allowed for expanded memory beyond 640KB. DOS 5 added improved memory management, a task switcher, a better DOS shell, support for 2.88MB floppy disks, and a command to "undelete" files. Versions of DOS are backward-compatible. Typically, programs designed for one version of DOS execute on all newer versions of DOS, as well.

FORMATTING DISKS WITH DOS

Addressable areas (clusters) must be defined before files can be saved on a disk. When you purchase a new disk, it is a generic disk. A disk can be used with different PCs, using a variety of different operating systems. Even with the same operating system data is recorded on different types of disks differently. Figure 3.4 shows you some of the different types of floppy disks used by DOS.

Figure 3.4
Floppy Disk Organization (Based on Disk Capacity)

	TOTAL DISK CAPACITY				
	360KB	720KB	1.2MB	1.44MB	2.88MB
Disk size	5 1/4"	3 1/2"	5 1/4"	3 1/2"	3 1/2"
Density type	double	double	quad (high)	quad (high)	ultra high
Sectors/track	9	9	15	18	36
Tracks/side	40	80	80	80	80
Bytes/cluster (allocation unit)	1024	1024	512	512	1024
Number of Disks Required to Copy 10MB of Data	29	15	9	8	4

The Formatting Process

Each blank disk (floppy or hard disk) must be prepared to record data according to the requirements of DOS and the type of disk. This process, called **formatting,** includes the following:

(1) DOS creates addressable areas of the disk called **clusters**. Because each disk drive and operating system has its own addressing scheme, this activity is mandatory before saving files. For example, each of the 40 tracks on one side of a 5 1/4-inch (360KB) floppy disk is divided into 9 sectors, for a total of 360 sectors. Each sector holds 512 bytes of data. A cluster is a corresponding track and sector on both sides of a disk, or 1024 bytes.

(2) DOS then checks every cluster on the new disk for damage. Clusters not acceptable for storing data are marked by DOS as being bad and are never used.

(3) DOS creates a disk directory and a File Allocation Table (FAT) on track zero of each disk. DOS uses the directory to keep track of file information. Cluster information is recorded in the FAT. The format process also updates track zero with a "boot record," to permanently identify the type of disk (e.g., 1.44MB).

(4) When you format a disk, DOS displays the status of your disk, including the number of bad sectors found. It's a good idea to replace floppy disks containing bad sectors. The cost of losing data is much higher than the cost of a new floppy disk.

HELP Command

Before we look at the FORMAT command, let's see how the HELP command can assist us in using DOS. If you are stuck trying to remember what DOS command to use, the **HELP** command may provide the information you need to jog your memory. When you enter HELP at the system prompt, DOS displays several screens of command summaries. It pauses at the end of each screen and waits for any keystroke to continue, as shown in Figure 3.5.

Figure 3.5
First HELP Screen

```
A>HELP

For more information on a specific command, type HELP command-name.
APPEND    Allows programs to open data files in specified directories as if
          they were in the current directory.
ASSIGN    Redirects requests for disk operations on one drive to a different
          drive.
ATTRIB    Displays or changes file attributes.
BACKUP    Backs up one or more files from one disk to another.
BREAK     Sets or clears extended CTRL+C checking.
CALL      Calls one batch program from another.
CD        Displays the name of or changes the current directory.
CHCP      Displays or sets the active code page number.
CHDIR     Displays the name of or changes the current directory.
CHKDSK    Checks a disk and displays a status report.
CLS       Clears the screen.
COMMAND   Starts a new instance of the MS-DOS command interpreter.
COMP      Compares the contents of two files or sets of files.
COPY      Copies one or more files to another location.
CTTY      Changes the terminal device used to control your system.
DATE      Displays or sets the date.
DEBUG     Runs Debug, a program testing and editing tool.
DEL       Deletes one or more files.
DIR       Displays a list of files and subdirectories in a directory.
---More---
```

Once you know what command you want to use, you can view the syntax of a command by entering the command name along with the HELP command. For example, suppose you wanted help with the FORMAT command. Figure 3.6 shows you what will be displayed when you enter the command **HELP FORMAT**. Experiment using the HELP command, first with just HELP and then with specific commands that interest you.

Figure 3.6
Syntax of the FORMAT Command Using HELP

```
A>HELP FORMAT
Formats a disk for use with MS-DOS.

FORMAT drive: [/V[:label]] [/Q] [/U] [/F:size] [/B | /S]
FORMAT drive: [/V[:label]] [/Q] [/U] [/T:tracks /N:sectors] [/B | /S]
FORMAT drive: [/V[:label]] [/Q] [/U] [/1] [/4] [/B | /S]
FORMAT drive: [/Q] [/U] [/1] [/4] [/8] [/B | /S]

  /V[:label]   Specifies the volume label.
  /Q           Performs a quick format.
  /U           Performs an unconditional format.
  /F:size      Specifies the size of the floppy disk to format (such
               as 160, 180, 320, 360, 720, 1.2, 1.44, 2.88).
  /B .         Allocates space on the formatted disk for system files.
  /S           Copies system files to the formatted disk.
  /T:tracks    Specifies the number of tracks per disk side.
  /N:sectors   Specifies the number of sectors per track.
  /1           Formats a single side of a floppy disk.
  /4           Formats a 5.25-inch 360K floppy disk in a high-density drive.
  /8           Formats eight sectors per track.

A>
```

The syntax of DOS commands used in this text will be much easier to follow than that in Figure 3.6. In an effort to simplify the process of understanding and using DOS, only the most common command parameters and options will be shown in this text. Additional information can be obtained with the HELP command, if needed.

FORMAT Command

Syntax: `[d:][path]FORMAT d: [/F:size] [/S]`

The **FORMAT** command prepares a disk in the designated drive to record data acceptable to DOS. All disks must be formatted before they can be used by DOS. During the format process of a 360KB disk, two write heads prepare 40 tracks (0–39) on each side for recording data. On other floppy disks, 80 tracks (0–79) are prepared. FORMAT examines each disk for defective sectors, making a note on the FAT of the bad sectors. The FORMAT command prompts you to enter a volume label to give your disk a name. In addition to establishing a disk directory and FAT, DOS randomly generates a disk serial number. This unique identifier does not change unless the disk is formatted again.

To make a disk bootable, use the **/S** option. It formats the disk and copies the two hidden system files (i.e., IO.SYS and MSDOS.SYS) and COMMAND.COM from a DOS disk. The slash (/) identifies a command option to DOS. The term "switch" is also used to represent a command option. If you enter the FORMAT command without specifying a disk, DOS will not automatically format the default disk. This feature keeps you from reformatting your DOS disk accidentally.

Another useful option is the **/F** option that specifies the size of the floppy disk to format. Use this option to format a 720KB disk in a 1.44MB floppy disk drive (i.e., /F:720). Due to the technical limitations of a low-density drive, you cannot format a 1.44MB disk in a 720KB disk drive. Figure 3.7 shows you a screen display of a format operation using the /F option. Refer to your DOS manual or HELP command for more information about this and other FORMAT options.

FORMAT produces an on-screen status report with the following statistics for the formatted disk: total disk space, sectors marked as defective (if any), space allocated to the system files (when /S is used), the amount of space left for other files, and information about the allocation units.

When you format a disk, all previously recorded data is destroyed. For this reason, many organizations hide their FORMAT command so it can't be used accidentally. Later in this text you will learn how to do this.

Figure 3.7
Screen Display of FORMAT with /F Option

```
A>FORMAT B:/S /F:720
Insert new diskette for drive B:
and press ENTER when ready...

Checking existing disk format.
Formatting 720K
Format complete.
System transferred

Volume label (11 characters, ENTER for none)? SOUTHWORTH

    730112 bytes total disk space
    119808 bytes used by system
    610304 bytes available on disk

      1024 bytes in each allocation unit.
       596 allocation units available on disk.

Volume Serial Number is 3A67-10FD

Format another (Y/N)?N


A>
```

Examples of usage:

A> FORMAT b:/s
(format the disk in Drive B so that it contains the system files, making it bootable)

A> format/s
(format the disk in the default drive with the system files)

B> A:Format
(format the disk in Drive B, the default drive)

A> format b: /f:720
(format the disk in Drive B as a 720KB disk)

Chapter 3

Review Questions

1. What is meant by the term "default drive" in DOS?
2. What do the standard device names CON and PRN represent?
3. Define the four parts of the full filename.
4. How is a filename extension identified by DOS?
5. What kind of file would likely have an extension of .SYS?
6. What are some common extensions for text files that are not executable, but may be displayed on the screen?
7. What are some common extensions for executable files?

8. In the command **DIR *.SYS**, what does the "*" represent?

9. Why is it important to name files correctly?

10. What is a date stamp in a disk's directory?

11. How do internal commands differ from external commands in DOS?

12. Give an example of an internal DOS command.

13. Give three examples of external DOS commands.

14. Why is the command **DIR** the same as the command **dir** in DOS?

15. When the command **HELP** is entered, what is displayed on the screen?

16. How can you view the syntax of the CHKDSK command in DOS?

17. What is a bad sector on a disk?

18. What is the purpose of the FORMAT command?

19. Why would you want to use the /S option with FORMAT?

20. What is the purpose of a status report when formatting a disk?

Chapter 3

Floppy Disk Lab Exercise

This exercise assumes that the system is already turned on. If it is not on, do a cold boot before you continue. This exercise is for computers with two floppy disk drives. The DOS disk should be in Drive A. If you are working with a hard disk system with a single floppy disk, skip ahead to the hard disk exercise. Otherwise, format a data disk to contain the DOS system files:

1. Enter **FORMAT B:/S** (remember, you can use lowercase characters).

2. Insert a blank disk in Drive B and press Enter.

3. Enter your name as the volume label (up to 11 characters with no special characters) when prompted to do so by DOS. You may use spaces in the label.

4. Enter **N** (or **n**) when prompted to format another disk. Figure 3.8 shows what the screen should look like when you finish formatting a 720KB blank floppy disk.

This completes the Chapter 3 floppy disk lab exercise. Remove your floppy disk(s) before you leave the computer.

Chapter 3
Hard Disk Lab Exercise

The DOS commands should already be loaded on your hard disk (C:). They should be stored in a separate subdirectory. For the examples in this book, we will assume that the subdirectory containing the DOS commands is named C:\DOS. If your computer is off, do a cold boot before proceeding.

Use the **DIR** command to view the files on the current directory. If the current directory does not contain your DOS commands, use the CD command to change to the appropriate directory (i.e., CD\DOS). Then format a data disk in Drive A to contain the DOS system files:

1. Enter **FORMAT A:/S** (remember, you can use lowercase characters).

2. Insert a blank disk in Drive A and press Enter to continue.

3. Enter your name as the volume label (up to 11 characters with no special characters) when prompted to do so by DOS. You may use spaces in the label.

4. Enter **N** (or **n**) when prompted to format another disk. Figure 3.7 shows what the screen should look similar to when you finish formatting a 720KB blank floppy disk.

This completes the Chapter 3 hard disk lab exercise. Remove your data disk before you leave the computer.

INTRODUCTION TO THE DOS SHELL

INTRODUCTION TO THE DOS SHELL

There has been a lot of discussion as to the merits of using the DOS shell. If you are a new user to DOS, you will likely find the DOS shell a handy feature. Those who are already familiar with entering commands at the system prompt may find it slow by comparison. The primary objective of this chapter is to introduce you to how the shell operates. Later chapters will include additional operations using the shell. After completing the hands-on work in this book, you will be able to form your own opinion about the shell.

The DOS shell is a user friendly alternative to entering commands at the system prompt. Information is displayed on the screen in a more visual form. Using a keyboard or a mouse, users simply point to select files and execute commands. The shell's purpose is to simplify the process of entering DOS commands.

DOS SHELL BASICS

The DOS shell uses a "windows" approach for displaying information on the screen. The greatest benefit of the windows approach is that users don't have to remember so much. For example, directory listings can be displayed to assist you in locating and selecting files to be processed. In addition, DOS commands can also be listed in a window and selected for execution without having to remember how to spell the command. The first screen you see when you use the DOS shell looks similar to Figure 4.1.

A **window** is a well-defined portion of the screen devoted to providing specific information to the user, such as listing files on a disk or listing a set of commands to execute. Like windows in a building, a window can be a single pane or it can be subdivided into multiple panes. With the DOS shell, the term "window" normally refers to a given pane, called an *area* or *box*. Some windows can be displayed next to each other; others can overlay portions of previous windows.

Figure 4.1
The DOS Shell Window

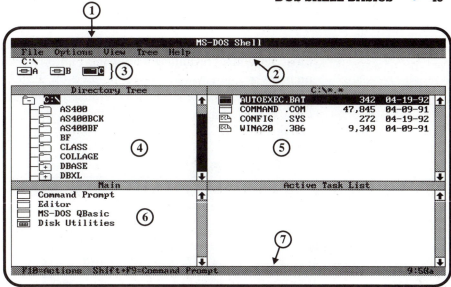

The Shell Window

The DOS shell window has seven major areas. These areas, noted in Figure 4.1, are as follows:

1. The *Title Bar* tells you that the shell is activated.

2. The *Menu Bar* displays the pull-down menu items that can be selected.

3. The *Drive List* shows you the possible disk drives you can select as the default drive alphabetically. As Figure 4.1 shows, the current default drive is highlighted (shown darker than the other drive letters). The data displayed in the remaining windows all relates to the selected disk drive.

4. The *Directory Tree* area displays the subdirectories on the default disk drive alphabetically. The root directory is initially highlighted as the current subdirectory. The + or − symbol next to a subdirectory name, indicates that it contains additional subdirectories.

5. The *File List* area, to the right of the Directory Tree window, lists the files in the current directory alphabetically. The first file in the directory is always selected and highlighted as the default file.

6. The *Main* program menu area shows you a list of program names installed to run from the shell, including the Command Prompt that lets you execute any DOS command from within the shell.

7. The *Status Bar* is used to display available keystrokes, the current system time, and any system messages.

Pull-down Menus The windows approach gives users a highly visible way to work. Most activities are initiated by using pull-down menus. A **pull-down menu** is a small window superimposed on the DOS shell screen. It lists a set of related actions or commands for a major type of activity. For example, Figure 4.2 contains the pull-down menu for file-oriented commands.

Figure 4.2
File Pull-down Menu

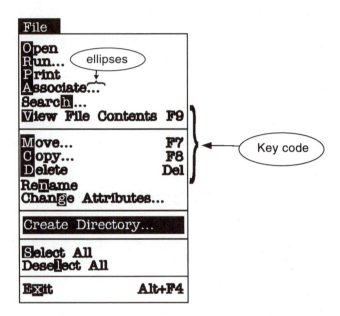

In the File menu in Figure 4.2, some commands have ellipses (. . .) next to their names. Ellipses indicate that the shell will require further information to execute the command. Some commands have a key code next to their name, such as F7 or F8. These keys are "short-cut" keys because they can be used to activate a command without first pulling down the command menu. Later we will discuss several other ways you can choose commands from a pull-down menu. If a command is shaded or missing, it is not currently available for use.

Dialog Boxes The DOS shell uses **dialog boxes** to request information it needs to carry out a task. Dialog boxes are like pull-down menus in that they overlay existing windows when activated. Figure 4.3 contains two dialog boxes used by the DOS shell. The first one is used to obtain file display options and the other to select a display color scheme.

Figure 4.3
Sample Dialog Boxes

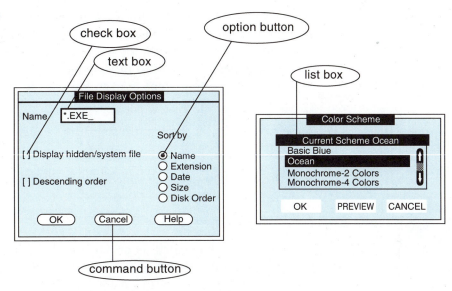

Most dialog boxes allow you to enter information in several ways. These types are found in dialog boxes:

- **Check box** A set of brackets forming a box containing an X or a blank space; it can be changed by selecting the box. You can select as many boxes with Xs as you need.

- **List box** A listing of choices that can be selected. Where permitted, you can select as many items as you need. Selected items become highlighted in the box.

- **Text box** A place where you can enter text from the keyboard. A row of dots identifies where the text is entered.

- **Option box** A listing of options, each with its own input area. You can select only one option at a time. When you select an option it displays a dot in the box.

- **Command buttons** A set of immediate actions to be carried out based on the information selected in the rest of the box. You can select only one command button (such as OK, Cancel, or Help) to be executed.

Selecting and Choosing

Working with the shell usually involves two interrelated processes, selecting and choosing. First you must **select** a desired file from a window on the screen. To select a file, use the arrow keys to point to (highlight) a file and then press the Enter key. To cancel a selection, simply select (highlight) another filename. Next, you can **choose** some type of action for the highlighted file by activating a pull-down menu. To activate a pull-down menu, press the F10 key and the first letter of the desired activity shown in the Menu bar at the top of the screen. For example, suppose you wanted to view the contents of a file. Conceptually, these are the four steps used to view a file:

1. Move to the File List window.

2. Select the file in the list, causing it to become highlighted.

3. Press F10 and F to activate the File pull-down menu.

4. Press V to choose the View option to display the highlighted file.

STARTING THE DOS SHELL

The shell might be started automatically, depending on how your system was configured when you booted DOS. Once you see a window displayed similar to Figure 4.1, the shell is active and ready for use. If the shell was not started automatically on your computer, start it by entering the following command at the system prompt:

```
C:\DOS> DOSSHELL
```

Note: If you have an EGA or VGA monitor, the shell may have been installed using the **graphics mode**, rather than the **text mode**. In the graphics mode, graphic images, called **icons**, appear in the window next to directory names and filenames.

USING THE SHELL WITH THE KEYBOARD

The Tab key is used to move from one window to another. The Esc key can be used at any time to exit from a menu or dialog box. Let's see how we can display the contents of the AUTOEXEC.BAT file, using the window in Figure 4.1.

1. To select a file, press the Tab key until the File List area is highlighted. The File List area is just to the right of the Directory Tree area, in the center of the screen.

2. Use the arrow keys to highlight the AUTOEXEC.BAT file. Use the Up arrow or Down arrow keys to scroll a line at a time. If a list is long, you can use the PgUp or PgDn keys to scroll through a greater number of lines.

3. To access the Menu Bar, press the F10 key, shown at the bottom

of the screen, for Actions. Because the menu you want is now highlighted, press the Enter key to activate the File pull-down menu. To activate any other menu, press the first letter of the menu name.

4. Press the underlined letter of the desired command. In this case, press V (for View) to display the contents of the highlighted file.

5. Press the Esc key to exit displaying the file.

USING THE SHELL WITH A MOUSE

If you have a mouse installed, you should see a mouse pointer on the screen. It will show as a small, lightly shaded rectangle if the shell was executed in the text mode. In the graphics mode, the mouse pointer displays as an arrow. If you can't locate the mouse pointer on the screen, try moving the mouse.

To select an item in a shell window, move the mouse pointer to the desired item and click on the item. Tap the left mouse button once to click on a selection. *To choose an action* you must double-click on a command. This requires that you tap the left mouse button twice, as quickly as possible, while pointing at the desired command. In addition to using the mouse to highlight files and actions, you can click on the scroll bars to scroll vertically through the contents of an area, such as a long File List.

To use the Menu Bar with a mouse, click on an item in the Menu Bar to display the pull-down menu and then click on the desired command. To cancel a pull-down menu, you may press the Esc key, click on the menu name again, or click anywhere outside the menu area.

CHANGING THE SHELL COLORS

Suppose you want to change the color scheme of the shell shown in Figure 4.3. The following demonstrates how you can select an item from a list using either the keyboard or a mouse:

KEYBOARD: Press the F10 key (Actions) and the letter O to select the Options menu. Choose O (C*o*lors) to see the Color Scheme dialog box. Highlight the desired color using the arrow keys, or press the first letter of a color. To preview the colors use the Tab key to select the Preview command button and press the Enter key. If you wish to skip the preview process, press the Enter key to execute the change. You can press the Esc key to cancel an operation.

MOUSE: Click on Options in the Menu Bar to display the Options menu. Click on Color Scheme and then on the desired color. Click on the appropriate command button to execute the command.

When you are satisfied that the color scheme has changed, use what you have learned to change it back to the way it was before you started this exercise. Otherwise, the color changes will remain for the next student when you exit the shell.

FORMATTING A DISK WITH THE SHELL

Let's see how the DOS shell can be used to execute a command you executed in Chapter 3 using the command line — the FORMAT command. Using either the keyboard or a mouse, do the following steps:

1. Move to the Main program menu area and activate the Disk Utilities submenu.

   KEYBOARD: Each time you press the Tab key, the next window area is selected (highlighted). Press the Tab key until the Main menu area is selected. Then press the Down arrow key three times to highlight Disk Utilities and press the Enter key.

   MOUSE: Move the mouse pointer to the Disk Utilities entry (not the icon) in the Main program menu area and double-click the left mouse button.

2. Activate the Format program from the Disk Utilities list.

   KEYBOARD: Press the Down arrow key five times (or press F) to highlight Format. Press the Enter key to select.

   MOUSE: Double-click on the Format entry (not the icon).

3. Provide the necessary parameters to execute the Format program.

   KEYBOARD: Enter the appropriate information to format a disk. For example, to format a bootable disk in Drive B, enter **B:/S** in the text box and press the Enter key. If the default disk drive (shown in the text box) is correct, press the Right arrow key to add the /S.

MOUSE: Enter data using the keyboard as above. Then, press the Enter key, or click on the appropriate command button.

4. Follow system directions to get back to the DOS shell Main menu.

RUNNING DOS COMMANDS FROM THE SHELL

There are several ways to run DOS commands from the shell. You have already seen how to run the Format program from the Disk Utilities menu. In addition, many DOS commands are included in the set of actions found in the Menu Bar. Here are two other ways to execute DOS commands:

1. If the command you want to run needs no parameters, you can choose it from the File List area. For example, let's run the CHKDSK command to see the status of the default disk. When CHKDSK is finished, press any key to return to the shell.

   KEYBOARD: Use the Tab key and arrow keys to select the DOS directory from the Directory Tree area and press Enter. In a similar manner, highlight the command CHKDSK.EXE from the File List area and press the Enter key to execute the highlighted command.

   MOUSE: Click on the DOS directory in the Directory Tree area. Then double-click on the CHKDSK.EXE command in the File List area.

2. If a DOS command you want to run requires additional parameters, and it is not included in the Menu Bar, you must execute it from the system prompt. This means you need to exit the shell, either permanently or on a temporary basis. The next section discusses the process of exiting the shell.

EXITING THE DOS SHELL

One way to exit the DOS shell is to activate the File pull-down menu and then select the Exit option. But a quicker method is to use one of the short-cut keys. The **F3** key can be pressed to leave the DOS shell immediately. Both of these methods will exit the shell permanently.

However, it is often advantageous to exit the shell on a temporary basis. This way, you can return to the shell more quickly, without requiring DOS to reload the shell. To leave the DOS shell temporarily and exit to the system prompt, press **Shift-F9**. To return to the shell, you must use the EXIT command.

Returning with the EXIT Command

The **EXIT** command is a DOS command that lets you return to a program (including the DOS shell) that you left temporarily. Many application programs let you "shell out" to the system prompt to execute DOS commands. This feature is especially common with word processing and spreadsheet programs. Entering EXIT at the DOS prompt returns you to the application program.

A word of caution is necessary, however. *If you temporarily exit from the shell, or any application program, you must return with the EXIT command.* If you left the shell using the Shift-F9 key and then entered DOSSHELL at the system prompt, there would be two copies of the shell loaded in memory. This could cause a lot of problems, so remember to keep track of how you exited the shell.

Using the Command Prompt

Another way of exiting the shell temporarily and executing DOS commands is through the Command Prompt entry in the Main program menu. Once this is selected, you can execute as many DOS commands as you like before returning to the shell with the EXIT command. To see how this works, do the following to get on-line help about the CHKDSK command.

KEYBOARD: Use the Tab key to select the Main program menu. If Disk Utilities is currently displayed in this area (from a prior operation), select Main to display the Main program menu. Press the Enter key to execute the highlighted item, Command Prompt. After entering **HELP CHKDSK** at the system prompt, remember to enter **EXIT** to return to the shell.

MOUSE: Click on the Main program menu. If Disk Utilities is currently displayed in this area (from a previous operation), click on Main to display the Main menu. Double-click on the Command Prompt entry. After entering **HELP CHKDSK** at the system prompt, remember to enter **EXIT** to return to the shell.

Several points of caution with regard to using the DOS shell are worth mentioning:

- From the Options Menu, you can choose Select Across Directories, which lets you select files in more than one directory at a time. *We recommend that you not enable this feature.* Because DOS displays only the filenames in the current directory, you won't be able to see all the filenames you selected. This can lead to inadvertently deleting identically named files from different directories.

- Whenever you exit from the DOS shell after making a change to the way it operates (such as changing the screen colors), DOS updates a system file (DOSSHELL.INI) with those changes. DOS uses this system file to tell it how to load and execute the DOS shell.

- Don't turn off the computer if you have temporarily left the shell and DOS is waiting for an EXIT command to return to the shell. Each time you leave the shell, DOS creates a temporary disk file to help it remember how to return to the same place in the shell. When it returns to the shell, DOS deletes the temporary file. If you turn the power off before DOS has a chance to delete these temporary files, they will occupy space on your disk needlessly.

Chapter 4

Review Questions

1. What is the major reason for using the DOS shell?
2. What is a benefit of using the "windows" approach with DOS?
3. Describe a pull-down menu.
4. What files are displayed in the File List at any given time?
5. Where is the Status Bar displayed when using the DOS shell?
6. What do ellipses (. . .) indicate on a pull-down menu?
7. What is the "short-cut" key to view the contents of a selected file? To delete a selected file?
8. What is the purpose of a dialog box?
9. What are the differences between a check box and an option box when using a DOS shell dialog box?
10. What is a text box?
11. Explain how the term "selecting" differs from the term "choosing" related to using the DOS shell.
12. How does the text mode differ from the graphics mode?
13. What is the function of the Tab key in the shell?
14. What is the function of the Esc key in the shell?
15. What is the function of the PgUp and PgDn keys in the shell?
16. What is the function of the F10 key in the shell?

17. Describe how a mouse is used to select an entry from a pull-down menu that is not currently displayed.

18. List three different ways to execute DOS commands using the shell.

19. How do you exit from the DOS shell permanently?

20. How do you exit from the shell temporarily and then return?

Chapter 4

Lab Exercises

If the DOS shell is not already active, enter the following command at the system prompt: **DOSSHELL**

1. This first exercise using the shell shows you how you can view the contents of a disk file. Normally, you will only want to view a "listable" text file, like AUTOEXEC.BAT or CONFIG.SYS. However, you can also view executable command files that include lots of strange-looking characters. Let's take a peek into the MORE.COM file. Because it is an executable file, only the right side of the screen will be somewhat readable. Use the PgUp and PgDn keys to browse through the contents of the file. Exit the View operation by pressing the Esc key.

KEYBOARD: Use the Tab key and arrow keys to select the DOS directory in the Directory Tree. Use the Down arrow key as many times as necessary to highlight the MORE.COM command in the File List. Now press F10 and F to activate the File menu. Choose V to view the selected file.

MOUSE: Click on the DOS directory in the Directory Tree. Then locate and click on the MORE.COM command in the File List. Click on File in the Menu Bar, then click on View in the File menu to view the highlighted file.

Now apply what you know to view some other files on the File List. View some listable files (those with a BAT, BAS, or TXT extension).

2. This exercise lets you display the File List in a different sequence. More than likely the current File list is displayed in filename sequence. Let's resequence the list by file size, so that the largest files are listed first (in descending order by size).

KEYBOARD: Press the F10 (Actions) key and the letter O to select the Options menu. Press the letter F to choose the File Display Options dialog box as shown in Figure 4.3. Press the Tab key twice to get to the Descending Order area. Press the

Spacebar to put an X in this selection. Press the Tab key once more to get to the Sort By area and use the Down arrow key to choose Size. Press the Enter key to execute the change.

MOUSE: Click on the Options menu in the Menu Bar. Then click on File Display Options followed by Descending Order and Size in the dialog box. Click on the OK command button to execute the change.

When you are satisfied that the order of the file list was changed, use what you have learned to change it back to the way it was before you started this exercise.

3. This exercise shows you how to execute a game that is both educational and entertaining. Applying what you learned in this chapter, do the following steps using either the mouse or the keyboard:

- Select the DOS directory from the Directory Tree area.

- Move to the File List area and locate a file called GORILLA.BAS. If it is not there, skip the rest of this exercise.

- Execute the QBasic program from the Main program menu area. Enter the program name **GORILLA** in the text box and press Enter to execute. Follow the directions given to play the game. When you are done, press the following keys to return to the shell window: Alt, F, X. Press the same keys again to return to the system prompt.

This is the end of the Chapter 4 Lab Exercises. We will be using the DOS shell throughout the remainder of the text.

INTERNAL COMMANDS

INTERNAL DOS COMMANDS

INTERNAL COMMANDS

This chapter covers 10 internal DOS commands often used with floppy disk systems. External commands are covered in Chapter 6. The discussion of each command includes the following items:

- The general syntax of the command.
- An explanation of the command parameters.
- Helpful options when using the command.
- Some examples of usage at the system prompt.
- Execution of the command from the DOS shell, if applicable.

In addition to the command name itself, DOS commands may have **parameters** showing the target of the command, as well as command options. Parameters are required with the COPY command, for example, to identify the file(s) to be copied. **Options**, often called switches, tell DOS how a command is to be executed. Command options are normally placed at the end of the command line. Parameters and options that apply primarily to hard disk systems will be covered later.

Optional parts of the command are shown enclosed in brackets. The brackets are not part of the command when entering it. Command options are preceded by a slash (/). Rarely used options have been intentionally omitted.

One command option, the /? option, is available for use in all DOS commands. This helpful option provides an on-line explanation for the given command. For example, the command **FORMAT /?** explains the syntax of the FORMAT command, including parameters and options. This is similar to entering HELP FORMAT.

A **delimiter** is a special character, or separator, used to separate parts of a DOS command. DOS uses a variety of delimiters, including spaces, commas, and semicolons. The examples in this text normally use spaces as delimiters. You may enter commands using any combination of uppercase or lowercase characters. You can stop execution before normal completion of commands in a variety of ways. For example, you can abort DOS commands while they are running by entering Ctrl-C (or Ctrl-Break). When commands display a large amount of output on the screen, Ctrl-S temporarily suspends, but won't cancel, the display. Pressing any key continues the display process. When software instructions direct you to "Press any key" this normally refers to any alphabetic (A–Z) key, numeric (0–9) key, or the spacebar. It does not refer to any of the special or control keys, such as Ctrl-C.

Invalid commands are rejected by DOS, resulting in an error message, such as **Bad command or filename**. You will see this message if the command cannot be found. If a filename is not on the disk specified, you will get a **File not Found** error message. When either of these error messages appear, re-enter the command correctly.

Because the space between the read/write heads and the surface of the disks is very small, any movement of the disk drive when the disk is operating can be very destructive. If you try to read a disk and no disk is in the designated drive, or the drive latch is open, you will get a **Drive not ready** error message. If track zero on a disk is bad and cannot store the FAT and directory, or the type of disk is not correct (like a high-density disk in a low-density drive), or you try to read data from a defective disk, DOS will display an error message.

Whenever you get an error message for a disk operation, DOS displays the message **Abort, Ignore, Retry, Fail?** If you cannot correct the problem, enter **A** to end (abort) the command that requested the disk operation. It is possible to ignore the problem by entering I, but this often causes additional problems and should be avoided. If you can correct the problem, such as closing a drive latch, fix the problem and enter **R** to retry the operation. The Fail option lets the disk operation fail, but does not abort the command that requested it. Usually, you should retry the disk operation if it is correctable. Otherwise, abort the command. Appendix C describes thirty additional DOS error messages.

INTERNAL DOS COMMANDS

Internal commands are part of the COMMAND.COM file loaded into RAM when DOS is booted. Therefore, you do not need to have a DOS disk in a disk drive when executing an internal command. Internal commands covered alphabetically in this chapter are as follows:

CLS — Clears the screen of all data.

COPY — Makes a copy of a disk file.

DATE — Displays and/or changes the system date.

DEL — Deletes a file from a disk.

DIR — Displays filenames from a disk.

REN — Changes the name of an existing file.

TIME — Displays and/or changes the system time.

TYPE — Displays the contents of a disk file.

VER — Displays the version number of DOS.

VOL — Displays a disk volume label.

CLS (Clear Screen) Command

Syntax: CLS

The **CLS** command clears all current characters from the monitor (display screen). It results in a blank screen with the system prompt and a blinking cursor in the upper left corner. There are no parameters or options for this command.

Example of Usage:

    A> CLS
(displays only the system prompt on the screen)

COPY Command

Syntax: COPY [d:]filename[.ext] [d:][filename[.ext]]
where the first filename is the source file and the second filename (optional) is the target file (the new file being created).

The **COPY** command lets you make copies of disk files to a formatted disk. It facilitates making backup copies of files without destroying existing files. Files on the target disk with the same name as the target file are replaced by the contents of the source file without warning.

If you omit the disk device designator (d:), DOS substitutes the default device. If you omit the optional target filename, the system uses the same filename as the source file. If the target filename is the same as the source file, and you do not specify a different disk drive, the COPY command is aborted with the following error message:

    File cannot be copied onto itself.
    0 file(s) copied

You can copy a group of files with the COPY command by using wildcard characters in the filenames. For example, to copy all files on the default Drive (A:) with an extension of TXT to Drive B, enter:

    A> COPY *.TXT B:

If you specify the source file as CON (for CONsole keyboard), the target file contains characters entered from the keyboard. Lines are limited to 127 characters each. You must press the Enter key at the end of each line. DOS uses Ctrl-Z to mark the end of a text file. To stop recording characters and insert the Ctrl-Z character, press the **F6** function key, <F6>, followed by the Enter key. Figure 5.1 shows you

Figure 5.1

Screen Display of the COPY CON Command

```
A>COPY CON TESTFILE.TXT
This is a test of the COPY CON command.
The Enter key is used to end each line.
This is the last line.^Z
        1 file(s) copied

A>
```

what the screen would look like if you used the COPY CON command to create a text file on the default disk drive.

COPY CON is used to type a small file of text, but it is not appropriate for larger files. DOS provides the EDIT command (covered in Chapter 9) for larger text files. Another DOS command to copy files (XCOPY) is covered in Chapter 6.

Examples of usage:

A> COPY *.* B:
(copies all files on the default disk, Drive A, to the disk in Drive B, without renaming files)

A> COPY *XYZ.* B:
(same as previous example — characters immediately following an * are ignored by DOS)

A> copy B:*.DOC
(copies all files on Drive B with an extension of DOC to the default disk)

A> Copy filea.doc b:filea.bak
(copies FILEA.DOC on Drive A to Drive B, renaming it FILEA.BAK)

A> copy con b:read.me
(creates a file on Drive B named READ.ME consisting of data entered from console)

```
A> COPY A:FILE*.DOC B:
```
(copies all files on Drive A with a DOC extension that begin with FILE to Drive B)

```
A> COPY FILEA.DOC PRN
```
(copies a text file, FILEA.DOC, to the printer)

```
A> copy con prn
```
(lets you use the keyboard like a typewriter, echoing keystrokes to the printer)

Using the DOS Shell to Copy Files

If you do not wish to experiment using the DOS shell, you can skip this section. Otherwise, for the COPY command (and others that follow) it is assumed that the DOS shell is already active. If not, enter the DOSSHELL command to install the shell, or the EXIT command to return to the shell. When the shell is activated, make sure the DOS commands are displayed in the File List area. If not, use the keyboard or the mouse to select the DOS directory from the Directory Tree area. Now you are ready to practice using the COPY command.

For this exercise, you will be making a backup copy of the ANSI.SYS file. If it is not included in the File List, pick another filename that *is* included. Do the following steps:

1. First, highlight the file you want to copy (ANSI.SYS) in the File List.

2. Display the File pull-down menu from the Menu Bar.

3. Select the Copy command from the File menu. It has ellipses next to the name, letting you know that additional information is required.

4. Because the "From:" file has previously been selected, you only need to enter the "To:" filename. The cursor indicates where you start typing text. If text already exists in the box, any text you type replaces it. Optionally, you can use the Left or Right arrow keys to move the cursor and insert or delete text at that point. For this exercise however, just type **ANSI.BAK** in the "To:" box.

5. When the text is typed, press the Enter key to execute the command. The backup file (ANSI.BAK) will not be included in the File List. If you change your mind, you can press the Esc key (or choose the Cancel command button) to exit any operation.

The File menu on the Menu Bar cannot be used for all copy operations. To use the COPY CON command, you must temporarily exit to the system prompt. Follow the steps below to create a text file from the keyboard as shown in Figure 5.1:

1. Select the Command Prompt entry from the Main program menu.

2. Enter the command **COPY CON TESTFILE.TXT** at the system prompt.

3. Enter the three lines of text following the COPY CON command in Figure 5.1, *pressing the Enter key after each line*.

4. Then press the **F6** function key and the **Enter** key on the next line.

The new file (TESTFILE.TXT) will now be included in the File List. If the list is in name sequence, you will likely have to scroll to near the end of the list to make sure it is there. In addition to the COPY CON command, the DATE, TIME, VER, and VOL commands (described below) are executed from the system prompt.

DATE Command

Syntax: DATE [mm-dd-yy] or [mm/dd/yy] or [mm.dd.yy]

The **DATE** command changes the system date. Values for day, month, and year are separated by hyphens, slash marks, or periods. If you specify a new date on the command line, the system is changed to that date. If you have a battery-operated clock-calendar in your PC, its date might also be changed by the DATE command. If you omit the date parameter, the system displays the current date and prompts you to enter a new date. Press the Enter key if you do not wish to change it. If you enter an invalid date, DOS prompts you to enter a correct date. The valid values for the DATE parameter are as follows:

mm = 1 to 12

dd = 1 to 31 (the maximum value is adjusted for each month by DOS)

yy = 80 to 99 (or, 1980 to 2099)

Examples of usage:

A> DATE 3/4/93
(changes the system date to March 4, 1993)

A> date 03-04-93
(also changes the system date to March 4, 1993)

A> DATE 11.15.1995
(sets the system date to November 15, 1995)

A> Date
(displays the current date and prompts you to change it)

DEL (Delete) Command

Syntax: DEL [d:]filename[.ext] [/P]

The **DEL** command deletes the specified disk file. If the drive designator is not specified, the default drive is assumed. You can use
wildcard characters in the filename and extension, but do so with
caution. If you use *.* to specify the file, all files on the designated
disk might be deleted. In this case, DOS gives you some measure of
protection against eliminating files by mistake; it pauses to ask you if
you are sure. If you are currently in another subdirectory, you can
delete all files in a subdirectory by specifying just the subdirectory
name.

You cannot delete read-only files without first changing the status
with the ATTRIB command, discussed in Chapter 6. Also, you cannot
delete hidden DOS files. Because the ERASE command is identical to
the DEL command, you may use either command.

If you use the **/P** option, DOS displays the name of the file to be
deleted and prompts you with the message **Delete (Y/N)**? Press Y to
confirm the deletion, N to cancel the deletion, or Ctrl-C to cancel the
DEL command when wildcard characters are used.

The term "delete" may be a little misleading, because files are not
physically erased from a disk. The DEL command flags the file's
entry on the disk directory as deleted, thereby allowing other data to
be written over the space it occupies. Technically, DOS releases space
in the FAT and replaces the first character of the filename in the
directory with an ASCII 229 character (ASCII stands for American
Standard Code for Information Interchange). This character is often
displayed as either a question mark or a pound sign by utility programs that let you "undelete" files.

Deleted files can normally be retrieved with the UNDELETE command, covered in Chapter 6. However, the MS-DOS reference manual
from Microsoft includes this important caution in the discussion of
the DEL command:

*Once you delete a file from your disk, you may not be able to
retrieve it. Although the* **undelete** *command can retrieve deleted*

files, it can do so with certainty only if no other files have been created or changed on the disk. If you accidentally delete a file that you want to keep, stop what you are doing and immediately use the **undelete** *command to retrieve the file.*

Examples of usage:

> A> DEL a:Memo.txt

(deletes file MEMO.TXT from Drive A)

> A> DEL memo.txt

(deletes file MEMO.TXT from the default drive)

> A> del *.txt

(deletes all files on the default drive with a TXT extension)

> A> DEL B:*.* /P

(deletes all files on Drive B, prompting you for confirmation before deleting each file)

> C:\DOS> DEL \TEMP

(deletes all files on the subdirectory C:\TEMP)

Using the DOS Shell to Delete Files

Using what you learned earlier, select the **ANSI.BAK** file (the backup copy) from the File List. Then choose the Delete command from the File pull-down menu and follow the instructions to delete ANSI.BAK.

DIR (Directory) Command

Syntax: DIR [d:][filename[.ext]] [/Ax] [/Oy] [/P] [/W]

The **DIR** command displays a directory, or listing, of the files on a specified disk. It includes the volume identification, the name of each file, the size in bytes of each file, the date and time each file was last modified, and the amount of free space left on the disk. If you do not designate a disk drive, DOS uses the default drive. If you specify a filename, the directory is limited to only that name. Because the filename can contain wildcard characters, the directory can be limited to a specific group of files.

Use the **/A** option to selectively list files based on file attributes. For example, because hidden files are not normally included on DIR listings, the command DIR /AH can be used to list hidden files. The following eight attribute values may be substituted for *x* in the above syntax of the DIR command:

A¦-A List files whose archive bits are (set on ¦ set off)

H¦-H List files that are (hidden ¦ not hidden)

R¦-R List files that are (read-only ¦ bit read only)

S¦-S List files that are (system files ¦ not system files)

You can use the **/O** option to sequentially list directory files in a variety of ways. The eight sequences (or orders) that may be substituted for *y* in the above syntax are as follows:

D¦-D Order by date (oldest to newest ¦ newest to oldest)

E¦-E Order alphabetically by extension (ascending ¦ descending)

N¦-N Order alphabetically by name (ascending ¦ descending)

S¦-S Order by file size (smallest to largest ¦ largest to smallest)

Many users like to use the **/ON** option to have their files listed in name sequence. The SET DIRCMD command can be used to change the default listing sequence for all directory listings. For example, to change the order of all directory listings to filename sequence, enter the following command:

```
A> SET DIRCMD = /ON
```

Figure 5.2

Screen Display of Sorted DIR with Pause (/P) Option

```
      Volume in drive C is PENWORTH
      Volume Serial Number is 16F1-A1C6
      Directory of C:\DOS

      .              <DIR>        01-01-80    10:57p
      ..             <DIR>        01-01-80    10:57p
      ANSI     SYS       9029 04-09-91     5:00a
      APPEND   EXE      10774 04-09-91     5:00a
      QBASIC   INI        175 03-28-92     6:29p
      ASSIGN   COM       6399 04-09-91     5:00a
      ATTRIB   EXE      15796 04-09-91     5:00a
      BACKUP   EXE      36092 04-09-91     5:00a
      CHKDSK   EXE      16200 04-09-91     5:00a
      COMMAND  COM      47845 04-09-91     5:00a
      COMP     EXE      14282 04-09-91     5:00a
      AUTO     BAT         85 04-17-92     1:41p
      COUNTRY  SYS      17069 04-09-91     5:00a
      DEBUG    EXE      20634 04-09-91     5:00a
      DELOLDOS EXE      17644 04-09-91     5:00a
      DISKCOMP COM      10652 04-09-91     5:00a
      DISKCOPY COM      11793 04-09-91     5:00a
      DISPLAY  SYS      15792 04-09-91     5:00a
      DOSHELP  HLP       5651 04-09-91     5:00a
      Press any key to continue . . .
```

Use the /P option to cause the computer to pause during the display of the directory when the screen is full. It continues displaying again after you press any key to signal you are ready to continue. Figure 5.2 shows what the screen might look like using the pause option with a directory in ascending sequence by filename. The first two <DIR> entries on the listing are system files used by DOS to keep track of subdirectory information on the disk.

Use the /W option to display the directory in a "wide" format. With this format, only the filenames are displayed in five columns across the screen. Figure 5.3 shows you what your screen might look like with the /W option.

Figure 5.3
Screen Display of Sorted DIR with Wide (/W) Option

```
    Volume Serial Number is 16F1-A1C6
    Directory of C:\DOS

[.]             [..]            ANSI.SYS        APPEND.EXE      OBASIC.INI
ASSIGN.COM      ATTRIB.EXE      BACKUP.EXE      CHKDSK.EXE      COMMAND.COM
COMP.EXE        AUTO.BAT        COUNTRY.SYS     DEBUG.EXE       DELOLDOS.EXE
DISKCOMP.COM    DISKCOPY.COM    DISPLAY.SYS     DOSHELP.HLP     DOSKEY.COM
DOSSHELL.COM    DOSSHELL.EXE    DOSSHELL.GRB    DOSSHELL.HLP    DOSSHELL.VID
DOSSWAP.EXE     DRIVER.SYS      EDIT.COM        EDIT.HLP        EDLIN.EXE
EGA.SYS         EMM386.EXE      EXE2BIN.EXE     EXPAND.EXE      FASTOPEN.EXE
FC.EXE          FDISK.EXE       FIND.EXE        FORMAT.COM      GORILLA.BAS
GRAFTABL.COM    GRAPHICS.COM    GRAPHICS.PRO    GWBASIC.EXE     HELP.EXE
HIMEM.SYS       JOIN.EXE        KEYB.COM        KEYBOARD.SYS    LABEL.EXE
LINK.EXE        LOADFIX.COM     MEM.EXE         MIRROR.COM      MODE.COM
MONEY.BAS       MONEY.DAT       MORE.COM        MSHERC.COM      NIBBLES.BAS
NLSFUNC.EXE     PACKING.LST     PHIND.BAT       PHONE.LST       PRINT.EXE
PRINTER.SYS     OBASIC.EXE      OBASIC.HLP      RAMDRIVE.SYS    README.TXT
RECOVER.EXE     REMLINE.BAS     REPLACE.EXE     RESTORE.EXE     DOSSHELL.INI
SETVER.EXE      SHARE.EXE       SMARTDRV.SYS    SORT.EXE        SUBST.EXE
SYS.COM         TREE.COM        UNDELETE.EXE    UNFORMAT.COM    XCOPY.EXE
XMA2EMS.SYS
          86 file(s)     2171667 bytes
                         1980416 bytes free

C>
```

Examples of Usage:

A> Dir
(displays a directory of all files on the default disk drive)

A> DIR B: /AH
(displays a directory of all hidden files on Drive B)

A> dir a:dog*.*
(displays directory of Drive A, of only those files with filenames that begin with DOG)

A> dir *.doc/o-d
(displays all .DOC files on Drive A in new-to-old sequence by date) **Note**: The slash serves as a command delimiter.

```
A> Dir b:/p
```
(displays the Drive B directory, pausing whenever the screen fills up)

```
A> dir /w
```
(displays filenames on the default drive in wide format)

```
A> DIR B: /ON/W/P
```
(displays filenames on Drive B, sequenced by filename, in wide format, pausing after each screen)

Using the DOS Shell for Directory Listings

Files in the File List can be displayed in different ways. Using the Options menu in the Menu Bar, the File Display Options dialog box can be selected. This dialog box lets you include hidden files in the File List. It also lets you choose the desired sequence for displaying the files.

REN (Rename) Command

Syntax: `REN [d:]filename[.ext] filename[.ext]`

The **REN** command changes the name of the file specified in the first parameter to the new name given in the second parameter. Wildcard characters are used in either parameter. A drive designator is not allowed in the second parameter. REN will not work if the new name already exists on the disk. REN lets you make disguised copies of important files. For example, a spreadsheet file called BUDGET.WK1 can be changed to WORK.EXE. A longer and commonly used spelling of the REN command is RENAME.

Examples of usage:

```
A> REN b:ltr1.doc ltr1.bak
```
(renames LTR1.DOC on Drive B to LTR1.BAK)

```
A> ren Ltr1.doc ltr1.bak
```
(renames LTR1.DOC on Drive A to LTR1.BAK)

```
A> Rename ltr1.doc *.bak
```
(renames LTR1.DOC on Drive A to LTR1.BAK — use of wildcard characters can save keystrokes)

```
A> REN *.TXT *.DOC
```
(renames all files with a TXT extension to an extension of DOC)

Using the DOS Shell to Rename Files

To rename a file, you must first select it in the File List. Then use the File pull-down menu to choose the Rename command. Follow the directions to change the name of the file you created previously, **TESTFILE.TXT**, to **NEWNAME.TXT**.

TIME Command

Syntax: `TIME [hh:[mm[:ss]]] [A |P]`

The **TIME** command changes the system time. If your PC has a battery-operated clock-calendar, the TIME command might automatically update its clock as well. You should keep the correct date and time on the system because it is recorded in the directory information of each file you save. If you omit all parameters, DOS displays the current system time and prompts you to change it. To leave the time unchanged, press the Enter key. If you enter an invalid time, the system prompts you to enter a new time.

The **A¦P** parameter specifies a.m. or p.m. respectively for the 12-hour time format. If you enter a valid 12-hour time without an A or a P, such as 8:30, DOS will default to a.m. Entries for hours, minutes, and seconds are delimited with a colon (:) or a period (.).

Examples of usage:

```
A> TIME 8:30
```
(changes the system time to 8:30 a.m.)

```
A> Time 14:15:35
```
(changes the time to 2:15 p.m. and 35 seconds)

```
A> time 2:15:35p
```
(also changes the time to 2:15 p.m. and 35 seconds)

```
A> TIME 2P
```
(changes the time to 2 p.m.)

```
A> time
```
(displays the current time and prompts you to enter a new time)

```
A> time 11.55.30
```
(changes the time to 11:55 a.m. and 30 seconds)

TYPE Command   Syntax: `TYPE [d:]filename[.ext]`

The **TYPE** command displays the contents of a human-readable file on the standard output device, normally the monitor. It does not alter files. This command is only meaningful when used with ASCII text files, not files that end with an extension of EXE or COM. Wildcard characters are not allowed. You can redirect the output to a file or to a printer, as shown in the last example below. Redirection of output is covered in Chapter 8.

Examples of usage:

`A> TYPE B:READ.ME`
(displays the contents of B:READ.ME on the monitor)

`A> type read.me`
(displays the contents of A:READ.ME on the monitor)

`A> TYPE AUTOEXEC.BAT >PRN`
(types the contents of AUTOEXEC.BAT on the printer)

Using the DOS Shell to Type (or View) Files

To send the contents of a text file to the printer, you would have to exit to the system prompt. However, it is relatively easy to display the contents of files on the screen. To view a file, it must first be selected in the File List. Then you can choose the View command from the File pull-down menu to display the contents. If the file is an executable file, only the right part of the screen may be readable. Use what you have learned to view the contents of a text file that you previously created and renamed, **NEWNAME.TXT**.

VER (Version) Command   Syntax: `VER`

The **VER** command displays the DOS version number on the screen, such as MS-DOS Version 5.0. This command is very useful if you don't know what DOS version was used to boot the system.

VOL (Display Volume Label) Command   Syntax: `VOL [d:]`

The **VOL** command displays the internal disk volume label and serial number of the designated drive, if they exist. Use this command to identify a disk rather than physically removing it from the drive. If you do not specify a drive, the default drive is assumed. Volume labels are created with the FORMAT command and changed with the LABEL command. The LABEL command is covered in the next chapter.

Examples of usage:

```
A> vol B:
```
(displays the volume label recorded on the disk in Drive B; if there is no label, it displays **Volume in drive B has no label**)

```
A> VOL
```
(displays the volume label of the default disk, Drive A)

Chapter 5

Review Questions

1. What is the function of brackets in this text for describing the syntax of DOS commands?

2. What is the function of the slash in this text for describing the syntax of DOS commands?

3. What is a delimiter and why is it required?

4. What does the message "Bad command or filename" mean?

5. Where are internal commands stored temporarily?

6. What DOS command erases information from the display screen?

7. What is the benefit of using wildcard characters in the COPY command?

8. What command lets you use the keyboard and printer as a typewriter?

9. What command removes the filename from the disk directory, but does not physically remove the file from the disk?

10. What command displays a directory listing on the screen with filenames in multiple columns?

11. What method is used to get a directory listing of a specific group of files?

12. What command will display all the hidden files on Drive A?

13. What command displays a directory listing of the default disk in sequence by file size (smallest to largest), pausing between screens?

14. What command displays a directory listing of Drive B in descending filename sequence for all files that are *not* read-only?

15. What happens if you include a disk drive designator on both parameters of the RENAME command?

16. What command changes the system time to 4 p.m.?

17. What type of file is considered "listable" with TYPE?

18. What command verifies the DOS version being used?

19. What command displays the internal label on a disk without getting a directory listing?

20. What command erases all the BAK files on Drive B, prompting you to confirm the deletion of each one?

Chapter 5

Floppy Disk Lab Exercises

Most of the following exercises can be executed from within the DOS shell. However, Exercises 4 and 5 require that you temporarily exit to the system prompt to enter the commands. Your instructor can decide which approach (the DOS shell or the command line) should be used to complete all the exercises.

1. Boot DOS (Drive A) and insert your data disk in Drive B. Enter **DIR B:** to see the files on Drive B. You should see the COMMAND.COM file that you created in Chapter 3 when you formatted your data disk.

2. In this exercise, you will use the COPY CON command to create a small text file.

   • Enter **COPY CON B:READ.ME** (or **copy con b:read.me**).

   • On the lines that follow, enter the following text, pressing the Enter key at the end of each line.

```
When entering DOS commands, the commands and parameters <Enter>
must be separated by delimiters. Delimiters are normally <Enter>
either a space or a comma. They can be used interchangeably <Enter>
within any command (i.e., COPY A:OLDFILE,B:). <F6><Enter>
```

   • If you have already ended a line that was in error by pressing the Enter key, you cannot correct the error at this time. You can start over completely by pressing Ctrl-C to cancel the COPY command and return to the system prompt.

   • After keying the line of text, press function key **F6** (to tell DOS you are done with the copy operation) and press Enter. The text you just keyed is stored on Drive B with the filename of

READ.ME. Figure 5.4 shows you the screen after you have completed the COPY CON command. The Ctrl-Z (^Z) was created when you pressed the F6 key to identify the end of the file.

Figure 5.4
Screen Display of
COPY CON

```
A>COPY CON B:READ.ME
When entering DOS commands, the commands and parameters
must be separated by delimiters.  Delimiters are normally
either a space or a comma.  They can be used interchangeably
within any command (i.e., COPY A:OLDFILE,B:).^Z
        1 file(s) copied

A>
```

3. Enter **COPY B:READ.ME B:TEST.1** and then **COPY B:READ.ME   B:TEST.2** to provide two more files to work with on Drive B. Then get a directory listing of Drive B in ascending sequence by file size (**DIR B:/OS**). Your screen should now look similar to Figure 5.5.

Figure 5.5
Screen Display of
Sorted Directory

```
A>COPY B:READ.ME B:TEST.1
        1 file(s) copied

A>COPY B:READ.ME B:TEST.2
        1 file(s) copied

A>DIR B:/OS

 Volume in drive B is SOUTHWORTH
 Volume Serial Number is 3A67-10FD
 Directory of B:\

READ     ME          223 07-27-92  10:24a
TEST     1           223 07-27-92  10:24a
TEST     2           223 07-27-92  10:24a
COMMAND  COM       47845 04-09-91   5:00a
        4 file(s)       48514 bytes
                       607232 bytes free

A>
```

4. Enter **REN B:TEST.2 TEST.3** to change the filename of TEST.2 on your data disk to TEST.3. Enter **DIR B:** to verify the name change. To simplify the commands in this step, you could have first changed the default disk to Drive B.

5. Enter **VOL B:** to see if your data disk has an internal volume label and serial number. If you did not enter a volume label when you formatted the disk, your data disk should not contain one.

6. Enter **VER** to see what DOS version was used to boot your system. Then, enter **DATE** and follow the system prompts to change the current system date. Then do the same for **TIME**. You only need to enter hh:mm (i.e., 13:45 or 1:45p) for the time, ignoring seconds.

7. Bonus exercise (requires application of prior learning):

   • Use the COPY command to copy B:TEST.1 to B:TEST.4, using a wildcard character for the target filename. Use DIR to confirm you have five files on Drive B.

   • Using the REN command, change all files on Drive B with a filename of TEST (any extension) to NEWNAME. Use wildcard characters whenever possible. Use the DIR command to confirm the results.

   • Now, copy all files on Drive B with a filename of NEWNAME to a filename of TEST, without changing the filename extension. Display a directory of the eight files on Drive B to confirm this operation. Finally, delete all files on Drive B with a filename of NEWNAME using the /P option. Your data disk now contains five files: COMMAND.COM, READ.ME, TEST.1, TEST.3, and TEST.4.

This completes the Chapter 5 floppy disk lab exercises. When you are done, be sure to remove your disk(s).

Chapter 5

Hard Disk Lab Exercises

Most of the following exercises can be executed from within the DOS shell. However, Exercises 4 and 5 require that you temporarily exit to the system prompt to enter the commands. Your instructor can decide which approach (the DOS shell or the command line) should be used to complete all the exercises.

1. Boot DOS (Drive C) and insert your data disk in Drive A. Enter **DIR** to make sure you are on the part of the hard disk containing the DOS commands. If you do not see the DOS commands displayed, enter

CD\DOS. Then enter **DIR A:** to see the files on Drive A. You should see the COMMAND.COM file created when you formatted your data disk in Chapter 3.

2. In this exercise, you will use the COPY CON command to create a small text file.

   - Enter **COPY CON A:READ.ME** (or **copy con a:read.me**).

   - On the lines that follow, enter the text shown in floppy disk exercise 2, pressing the Enter key at the end of each line.

   - If you have already ended a line that was in error by pressing the Enter key, you cannot correct the error at this time. You can start over completely by pressing Ctrl-C to cancel the COPY command and return to the system prompt.

   - After keying the last line of text, press function key F6 (to tell DOS you are done with the copy operation) and press Enter. The text you just keyed is stored on Drive A with the filename of READ.ME. Figure 5.4 above shows you the screen after you have completed the COPY CON command. The Ctrl-Z (^Z) was created when you pressed the F6 key to identify the end of the file.

3. Enter **COPY A:READ.ME A:TEST.1** and then **COPY A:READ.ME A:TEST.2** to provide two more files to work with on Drive A. Then get a directory listing of Drive A in ascending sequence by file size (**DIR A:/OS**). Your screen should now look similar to Figure 5.5.

4. Enter **REN A:TEST.2 TEST.3** to change the filename of TEST.2 on your data disk to TEST.3. Enter **DIR A:** to verify the name change. To simplify the commands in this step, you could have first changed the default disk to Drive A.

5. Enter **VOL A:** to see if your data disk has an internal volume label and serial number. If you did not enter a volume label when you formatted the disk, your data disk should not contain one.

6. Enter **VER** to see what DOS version was used to boot your system. Then, enter **DATE** and follow the system prompts to change the current system date. Then do the same for **TIME**. You only need to enter hh:mm (i.e., 13:45 or 1:45p) for the time, ignoring seconds.

7. Bonus exercise (requires application of prior learning):

   - Use the COPY command to copy A:TEST.1 to A:TEST.4, using a wildcard character for the target filename. Use DIR to verify you have five files on Drive A.

- Using the REN command, change all files on Drive A with a filename of TEST (any extension) to NEWNAME. Use wildcard characters whenever possible. Use the DIR command to confirm the results.

- Now, copy all files on Drive A with a filename of NEWNAME to a filename of TEST, without changing the filename extension. Display a directory of the eight files on Drive A to confirm this operation. Finally, delete all files on Drive A with a filename of NEWNAME using the /P option. Your data disk now contains five files: COMMAND.COM, READ.ME, TEST.1, TEST.3, and TEST.4.

This completes the Chapter 5 hard disk lab exercises. When you are done, be sure to remove your data disk.

EXTERNAL DISK COMMANDS

EXTERNAL COMMANDS

ATTRIB (Attribute) Command

CHKDSK (Check Disk) Command

DISKCOPY Command

LABEL (Volume Label) Command

RECOVER Command

UNDELETE Command

XCOPY Command

Memory is very precious on a computer, so only the most commonly used DOS commands are internal commands, commands that are part of COMMAND.COM and are loaded into RAM when DOS is booted (see Chapter 5). The rest of the DOS commands, called **external commands,** remain on a disk and must be loaded each time they are executed.

Therefore, all external commands have an optional disk drive designator, which DOS uses to find them. For example, suppose the default disk is Drive B and DOS is loaded in Drive A. To execute CHKDSK, enter **A:CHKDSK.** If the designator (i.e., A:) is omitted, DOS looks for the external command on the default drive. The external commands covered in this chapter include:

   *****ATTRIB** — Sets the file attributes of a disk file.

   CHKDSK — Provides a disk status report and fixes corrupted disks.

   *****DISKCOPY** — Makes a duplicate copy of a floppy disk.

   LABEL — Creates, changes, or deletes a disk volume label.

   RECOVER — Recovers a file with defective sectors.

   *****UNDELETE** — Retrieves accidentally deleted disk files.

   XCOPY — Expanded version of the COPY command.

Note: Commands marked with an asterisk (*) can be executed using the DOS shell.

EXTERNAL COMMANDS

**ATTRIB
(Attribute)
Command**

Syntax: `[d:][path]ATTRIB [+A¦-A][+H¦-H][+R¦-R]`
          `[d:]filename[.ext] [/S]`

The **ATTRIB** command sets file attributes, including archive, hidden, and read-only status. The drive designator [d:] is required if the ATTRIB command is not on the default drive. The [path] is required for all external commands if the command is not in the current directory. If you enter ATTRIB with no parameters to set attributes, DOS displays the attribute status of the files or disk specified. You may use wildcard characters in the filenames. The **/S** option sets file attributes on a group of directories. It is used with hard disk systems containing subdirectories.

The read-only attribute protects files in a shared or networked environment where you don't want others accidentally destroying your files. If you have important files that you don't want changed, you can add a degree of safety by marking them as read-only with ATTRIB. Enter **+R** to set the read-only status on and **-R** to remove it. Files identified as read-only cannot be altered without resetting their status with the ATTRIB command.

Use **+A** or **-A** to set the archive attribute. Commands like BACKUP and XCOPY can selectively copy files that have the archive attribute on (+A). If you wish to keep certain files from displaying on the normal directory listings, use **+H** to keep them hidden. The **-H** parameter removes the hidden status.

Examples of usage:

```
A> ATTRIB +r b:filea.txt
```
(sets FILEA.TXT on Drive B to read-only status)

```
A> attrib -r B:*.txt
```
(sets all files on Drive B with a TXT extension so they are *not* read-only files)

```
A> B:attrib +h read.me
```
(hides READ.ME on the default drive, using a DOS disk in Drive B)

```
A> ATTRIB B:READ.ME
```
(displays the file attributes of READ.ME on Drive B)

```
A> ATTRIB B:
```
(displays the attributes of all files on Drive B)

```
A> ATTRIB +R A:COMMAND.COM
```
(helps to protect your COMMAND.COM file from being adversely affected by some computer viruses by setting it to read-only)

```
A> attrib +a b:memo.*
```
(turns on the archive attribute for all files on Drive B named MEMO)

Using the DOS Shell to View and/or Change File Attributes

To *view attributes* of a file that has been selected and highlighted in the File List, choose the **Show Information** option from the **Options** pull-down menu. You can exit from the dialog box by pressing the Esc key.

To *change attributes* of the selected file, choose the **Change Attributes** option in the **File** pull-down menu. Exit from the dialog box, executing the changes, by choosing the OK command button. If you exit with the Esc key, no changes will be made.

Using what you have learned, use the DOS shell to do the following practice exercises:

1. Move to the File List area and select the Format command.

2. Using the Show Information option, view its attributes.

3. Using the Change Attributes option, change the Format command to be a read-only file. Then view its attributes again.

Selecting More Than One File from a File List

There are times that you may wish to execute a command on a group of files without using wildcard characters. The DOS shell lets you do this within the set of files displayed in the File List as follows:

1. To select all the files in the File List, choose the Select All option in the File menu.

2. To select a subset of two or more files that are listed together (in sequence), you must use the Shift key. Highlight the first file in the sequence and hold down the Shift key as you highlight the rest of the files you want selected, one at a time. This approach works with a mouse, as well as with the Up and Down arrow keys.

3. The process of selecting two or more files that are not in sequence is a bit more complicated using the keyboard.

    KEYBOARD: You must press the Shift-F8 combination key after selecting the first file in the File List. The message "Add" will then be displayed in the Status Bar. Use the arrow keys to locate the next file and select it by pressing the spacebar. After all files have been selected, press Shift-F8 to exit from the "add mode."

    MOUSE: Press and hold down the Ctrl key (continuously) while you click the name of each file you want to select, including the first file.

After performing the desired actions for a group of files, you may wish to "deselect" them before doing your next operation. To do this, choose the **Deselect** option from the **File** pull-down menu.

CHKDSK (Check Disk) Command

Syntax: `[d:][path]CHKDSK [d:][filename[.ext]] [/F] [/V]`

The **CHKDSK** command produces a disk status report for a specified disk and lists the memory status of the system. The **/F** option fixes problems in the File Allocation Table. The **/V** option displays the full filenames of all files on a specified drive. After checking the disk, CHKDSK displays any error messages, followed by a status report. Figure 6.1 is an example of a CHKDSK report for a 720KB floppy disk:

Figure 6.1

Sample CHKDSK Report

```
Volume DATADISK    created 10-07-1992 8:35a

Volume Serial Number is 3765-13EC

    730112 bytes total disk space
     71680 bytes in 2 hidden files
    284672 bytes in 18 user files
    373760 bytes available on disk

      1024 bytes in each allocation unit
       713 total allocation units on disk
       365 available allocation units on disk

    655360 bytes total memory
    616080 bytes free
```

The two hidden files in the status report represent the DOS system files that are hidden from normal directory lists. The bottom portion of the report represents the memory status of a computer with 640KB of RAM. The difference between the 655,360 bytes of total memory shown above and the 616,080 bytes free is about 39KB. That is the amount of RAM space allocated to the resident portion of DOS and the space required to load and execute CHKDSK.

A file is written to contiguous clusters (allocation units) if the first unallocated space is big enough to hold it. Otherwise, DOS uses whatever clusters it finds to store a file, skipping over allocated clusters. Consequently, files can easily become fragmented.

If you specify a filename or group of files, CHKDSK displays the number of noncontiguous areas occupied by the file(s). Wildcard characters may be used in the filename. For example, you can use *.* to determine the extent of file fragmentation on a given directory of a disk. The COPY command can be used to rewrite fragmented files to a newly formatted disk. This process is recommended to improve access speed.

Lost allocation clusters are parts of files shown as allocated in the File Allocation Table (FAT), even though they are absent in the directory. This discrepancy occurs because of some malfunction during the file saving process. It can happen with a loss of power or by resetting the computer during a disk write operation.

You can use the /F option to combine lost clusters on a disk into a file named FILEnnnn.CHK, where nnnn is a unique number. This is a good command to use periodically. When the FAT is corrupted, it cannot accurately track files on disk. Whenever CHKDSK /F finds any lost clusters, you will see an error message similar to this:

```
6 lost clusters found in 2 chains.
Convert lost chains to files (Y/N)?
```

In this example, CHKDSK determined that lost data came from two different files (or two parts of the same file). If you respond Y, a file with a CHK extension is created for each chain. If a CHK file created by CHKDSK is listable, you can use TYPE to view the lost data. After identifying the lost data, you should delete all CHK files to make room for other files on the disk. If you respond N, DOS removes the lost clusters, but it doesn't save the contents for you to see.

When you use CHKDSK *without the /F option* and errors are detected, you must run it again with the /F option to fix those errors. If CHKDSK reports problems, fix them before continuing to use the disk. The problems can only get worse if you wait. We recommend you use CHKDSK whenever the following conditions occur:

- Unexpected data appears within a file or on a directory listing.

- A program fails to run as it should.

- You suspect disk damage after major problems, such as a power failure or a system lockup.

Examples of usage:

A> CHKDSK

(displays a status report for the default drive)

A> chkdsk /f

(displays a status report for Drive A and fixes any errors found in the FAT)

A> b:chkdsk a:*.*

(loads CHKDSK from Drive B, displays a status report for Drive A, and lists any fragmented files found on Drive A)

A> chkdsk B:read.me

(displays a status report for Drive B and displays the number of noncontiguous areas contained in READ.ME)

C:\WORD\FILES> CHKDSK *.*

(displays a status report identifying any fragmented files in the C:\WORD\FILES subdirectory)

DISKCOPY Command

Syntax: [d:][path]DISKCOPY d: d:

Unlike the COPY command, which duplicates files, DISKCOPY duplicates floppy disks. The **DISKCOPY** command copies the contents of an entire floppy disk, track by track and sector by sector, to another disk of the same density. If the source disk has a volume serial number, DOS creates a different one for the target disk. If you specify only one drive as the source and target disk, DOS tells you when to switch disks. Unlike the COPY command, DISKCOPY duplicates system and hidden files. It also duplicates fragmented files, without removing the fragmentation. Because DISKCOPY destroys all files on the target disk, you should use this command only when you do not wish to save any of the files on the target disk.

DISKCOPY is one of the few commands other than FORMAT that can format a disk if required. When duplicating a disk to an unformatted one, any bad sectors on the target disk (those normally bypassed by using COPY) may be overwritten during DISKCOPY, resulting in lost data. In addition, any bad sectors noted on the source disk are marked as bad on the target disk. Error messages display when errors are detected during the copy operation. To verify that a disk created with DISKCOPY is identical to the source disk, you can use the DISKCOMP command (consult your DOS manual) to compare the disks.

Examples of usage:

```
A> DISKCOPY A: B:
```
(makes an exact copy of the disk in Drive A onto a disk in Drive B; the target disk does not need to be previously formatted)

```
A> diskcopy a:
```
(makes an exact copy of the first disk inserted in Drive A onto a second disk to be inserted into Drive A)

Using the DOS Shell to Copy Disks

To copy one floppy disk to another of the same type, you first need to access the Disk Utilities entry in the Main program menu area. Then choose Disk Copy and follow the directions to copy the disks.

LABEL (Volume Label) Command

Syntax: `[d:][path]LABEL [d:] [volume label]`

The **LABEL** command lets you create, change, or delete a volume label on a disk. It is a good idea to label your disks internally. Then you can identify them using the VOL command without having to remove the disk from a drive to read an external label attached to the disk. DOS also displays the volume label when you run the DIR, CHKDSK, or TREE commands. If you do not specify a volume label, DOS displays the current label. It then prompts you to enter a label or press the Enter key to delete the current label.

Examples of usage:

```
A> Label b:fred
```
(creates a volume label of FRED on the disk in Drive B)

```
B> A:LABEL FRED
```
(also creates a volume label of FRED on the disk in Drive B)

```
A> LABEL
```
(displays the current volume label on the default drive and prompts you to modify it)

RECOVER Command

Syntax: `[d:][path]RECOVER [d:]filename[.ext]`

The **RECOVER** command lets you reconstruct a file from a disk that has defective sectors. Wildcard characters are not allowed with the RECOVER command. You can use it to recover a file containing bad sectors, minus the data in the bad sectors. If the recovered file is not an executable file, you can use EDIT (covered in Chapter 9) to replace the data that could not be recovered. Or, you may be able to use an application program, such as a word processing program, to replace the missing data. Other files should be restored from a backup copy.

Examples of usage:

    A> RECOVER b:memo.txt
(recovers a file called MEMO.TXT on Drive B)

    A> recover config.sys
(recovers the CONFIG.SYS file on Drive A)

UNDELETE Command

Syntax: `[d:][path]UNDELETE [[d:]filename[.ext]] [/LIST]`

The **UNDELETE** command restores files deleted with the DEL command. You can selectively undelete files by specifying the filename(s). Wildcard characters are permitted. If no filenames are supplied, UNDELETE lets you restore all deleted files, prompting you for confirmation on each file. The /LIST option lists deleted files, but it does not undelete any files.

UNDELETE only restores deleted files if the space freed up in the FAT has not yet been used by other files. *Whenever you accidentally delete a file, use the UNDELETE command immediately, before the data gets overwritten.* Figure 6.2 shows you a screen display of an UNDELETE operation.

Figure 6.2

Screen Display of an UNDELETE Process

```
A>UNDELETE

Directory: A:\
File Specifications: *.*

    Deletion-tracking file not found.

    MS-DOS directory contains    1 deleted files.
    Of those,    1 files may be recovered.

Using the MS-DOS directory.

    ?ESTFILE TXT    104  7-27-92 10:15a  ...A  Undelete (Y/N)?Y
    Please type the first character for ?ESTFILE.TXT: T

File successfully undeleted.


A>
```

Examples of usage:

```
A> undelete b:/list
```
(lists any deleted files on Drive B)

```
A> UNDELETE B:*.DOC
```
(lets you restore any deleted DOC files on Drive B)

Using the DOS Shell to Undelete Files

The Undelete option is included in the Disk Utilities submenu in the Main program menu area. It can be used to identify the deleted files in the currently selected directory (the one highlighted in the Directory Tree). The default command parameter in the text box is the /LIST option. Generally, you should execute the command with this option before attempting to undelete a file.

To undelete a file in the current directory, enter the appropriate parameter into the text box, such as *.* or *.BAK. If the undelete process was successful, you should tell DOS to reread the disk's directory to include the undelete file(s) on the File List. This is done by choosing the Refresh option on the Tree pull-down menu.

Possibly, there is a deleted file on your current DOS directory. Use the Undelete option (with /LIST as the parameter) to find out which files on the DOS directory have a deleted status. After identifying the deleted file(s), use the Undelete option to undelete one of them. Then refresh the screen to cause the undelete file(s) to be included in the File List.

XCOPY Command

Syntax: `[d:][path]XCOPY [d:]filename[.ext]`
`[[d:]filename[.ext]] [/M] [/P] [/S]`

The **XCOPY** command is used to selectively copy files and directories, including any lower-level subdirectories and their files. The first filename in the syntax represents the source file(s), and the second filename identifies the target filename(s). If you do not specify a disk drive or path, DOS uses normal default values. If you do not specify a target file, DOS copies to the default directory using the same filenames as the source files. If the specified path does not exist on the target disk, XCOPY creates the directories as it copies files to those directories.

The source can include multiple files with the use of wildcard characters. Like the COPY command, it will not copy hidden files or replace matching read-only files. Unlike COPY, XCOPY will not copy to or from devices like PRN and CON.

XCOPY uses an effective buffering technique to copy files. Multiple files are read into RAM (as much as RAM will hold) and then copied to the target disk as a group. When you have a large number of files to copy, this approach is faster than using COPY, which copies only one file at a time. The execution options provided give XCOPY power and flexibility.

The /M option copies only files that have their archive attribute set on (those that have not yet been backed up). Once copied it turns off the archive attribute, as does the BACKUP command (Chapter 7). It makes it easy to copy many files onto multiple backup disks. You can set the archive attribute on files by using the ATTRIB command with the +A parameter. When you use XCOPY to copy all the files on the disk with /M, as each backup disk fills up, the source files will have their archive attribute set off. You can repeat the same XCOPY command until no more source files have their archive attribute on.

The /P option prompts you with a message allowing you to selectively confirm whether you want to copy each file. This option lets you issue a single XCOPY command with wildcard characters and then selectively copy desired files from that set of files.

The /S option copies files from directories, including all lower-level subdirectories. *If you omit this option, DOS copies only files in the single directory specified.* If the source is a directory, then DOS makes the target a directory. If the target directory does not exist, DOS automatically creates one.

Examples of Usage:

    A> XCOPY \word*.DOC b:\bkup\

(copies all files in the WORD directory on the default disk to a directory on Drive B named \BKUP, without changing any filenames)

    C:\DOS> xcopy *.* b:/m/s

(copies all files in all directories and subdirectories of Drive C with their archive attribute ON to Drive B)

```
C:\DOS> XCOPY A:*.* B:*.BAK /S/P
```
(copies all files on Drive A, from all directories, to Drive B, changing the extensions to BAK and pausing to confirm that each file should be copied)

```
C:\LOTUS> XCOPY *.WK? A:/S
```
(copies all the spreadsheet files on the default directory, and its lower directories, to Drive A)

Chapter 6
Review Questions

1. What distinguishes external commands from internal commands?

2. What command sets B:MEMO.DOC to read-only status?

3. What command shows you the file attributes for all files on Drive A?

4. What are the hidden files you would expect to find on a system disk?

5. What command protects the COMMAND.COM file from being changed?

6. What command turns off the archive attribute for all BAK files on Drive B?

7. Describe the process to select more than one file in a File List when using the DOS shell with a mouse.

8. How can you determine the amount of file fragmentation on a disk?

9. What command fixes a corrupted FAT?

10. Define a "lost allocation cluster" on a disk.

11. What are the primary differences between using the COPY command and using the DISKCOPY command?

12. How can the internal volume label be changed without reformatting the disk?

13. After you reconstruct an ASCII file from a disk with defective sectors, what must you do before you can use it correctly?

14. What is contained in a file called FILE0001.CHK?

15. What command lists all the deleted files on Drive B?

16. Under what circumstances would you be unable to successfully undelete a previously deleted file?

17. What command restores B:MEMO.DOC if you accidentally delete it?

18. In what ways are the COPY command and the XCOPY command the same?

19. In what ways are COPY and XCOPY different?

20. What are the benefits of placing all of an application's data files in separate subdirectories?

Chapter 6

Floppy Disk Lab Exercises

Most of the following exercises can be executed within the DOS shell. Your instructor can decide which approach (the shell or command line) should be used to complete these exercises.

1. Boot DOS (Drive A) and insert your data disk into Drive B. Enter **DIR B:** to verify the contents of Drive B. Enter **ATTRIB +R B:TEST.3** to set a file to read-only status. Enter **ATTRIB B:*.*** to verify that it was changed correctly. If done correctly, TEST.1 and TEST.4 will not indicate a read-only status and TEST.3 will be a read-only file. An R is displayed to the left of read-only filenames. An S indicates a system file. Figure 6.3 shows you what the screen should look like at this point in the exercise.

2. If you are not certain about the syntax of a DOS command, you can get help by entering the command name with the /? option. Use this option with several of the external commands discussed in this chapter (for example, **ATTRIB /?**).

Figure 6.3
Screen Display of DIR and ATTRIB

```
    Volume in drive B is SOUTHWORTH
    Volume Serial Number is 3A67-10FD
    Directory of B:\

COMMAND  COM    47845 04-09-91    5:00a
READ     ME       223 07-27-92   10:24a
TEST     1        223 07-27-92   10:24a
TEST     3        223 07-27-92   10:24a
TEST     4        223 07-27-92   10:24a
         5 file(s)        48737 bytes
                         606208 bytes free


A>ATTRIB +R B:TEST.3

A>ATTRIB B:*.*
  A   SHR     B:\IO.SYS
  A   SHR     B:\MSDOS.SYS
  A           B:\COMMAND.COM
  A           B:\READ.ME
  A           B:\TEST.1
  A    R      B:\TEST.3
  A           B:\TEST.4

A>
```

3. To give a disk on Drive B a volume label, enter **LABEL B:** and follow the system prompts to enter a label of up to 11 characters (i.e., DATADISK). Enter **VOL B:** to verify the new volume label. Does your DOS disk have a volume label? Use the VOL command to check, but don't try to change it.

4. Enter **ATTRIB +H B:TEST.*** to hide all the files on Drive B that have a filename of TEST. Enter **DIR B:** to display a directory listing of Drive B without including these hidden files. Now enter the same command with the **/AH** option to display only the hidden files. Enter **ATTRIB -H B:TEST.*** to reset the hidden attribute so these files will normally be included in directory listings.

5. Enter **CHKDSK** to get a status report of the default drive (A:). Then enter **CHKDSK B:*.*** to get a status report of your data disk, directing the system to check for any fragmented files. Figure 6.4 shows the display screen after running CHKDSK. Your display screen should look similar to this one.

6. Delete all the TEST files on Drive B. Enter **UNDELETE B:/LIST** to see what files were deleted on Drive B. Your screen should look something like Figure 6.5. Then, enter **UNDELETE B:TEST.*** to restore them. Follow the instructions to undelete files and restore the first character of the filename (T). Finally, get a directory listing of Drive B to verify that the files were restored correctly.

Figure 6.4

Screen Display of CHKDSK

```
A>CHKDSK B:*.*

Volume DATADISK      created 07-27-1992 10:37a
Volume Serial Number is 3A67-10FD

    730112 bytes total disk space
     71680 bytes in 2 hidden files
     52224 bytes in 5 user files
    606208 bytes available on disk

      1024 bytes in each allocation unit
       713 total allocation units on disk
       592 available allocation units on disk

    655360 total bytes memory
    520800 bytes free

All specified file(s) are contiguous

A>
```

Figure 6.5
Screen Display of UNDELETE

```
A>DEL B:TEST.*

A>UNDELETE B:/LIST

Directory: B:\
File Specifications: *.*

    Deletion-tracking file not found.

    MS-DOS directory contains    2 deleted files.
    Of those,    2 files may be recovered.

Using the MS-DOS directory.

        ?EST    1       223  7-27-92 10:24a  ...A
        ?EST    4       223  7-27-92 10:24a  ...A

A>
```

7. Bonus exercise (requires application of prior learning):

   - Copy B:TEST.1 to B:TEST.ROF. Set the new file to read-only status and try to delete it. Then, reset the read-only attribute to allow writing to the file. Set the hidden file attribute of B:TEST.ROF to make it a hidden file and use the DIR command to verify that it is hidden. Before you continue, do whatever is required to delete B:TEST.ROF, and then restore it with the UNDELETE command.

   - Use the LABEL command to eliminate the volume label on your data disk. Use the VOL command to confirm that it is no longer there. Then change it back to its previous value. Use the DIR command to confirm the change. This demonstrates that there are at least three commands that display a disk's volume label. What is another DOS command that displays the label?

   This concludes the Chapter 6 floppy disk lab exercises. When you are finished, remove your disk(s).

Chapter 6
Hard Disk Lab Exercises

Most of the following exercises can be executed within the DOS shell. Your instructor can decide which approach (the shell or command line) should be used to complete these exercises.

1. Boot DOS (Drive C) and insert your data disk into Drive A. If you are not at the DOS portion of the hard disk, enter **CD\DOS.** Enter **DIR**

A: to verify the contents of Drive A. Enter **ATTRIB +R A:TEST.3** to set a file to a read-only status. Enter **ATTRIB A:*.*** to verify that it was changed correctly. If done correctly, TEST.1 and TEST.4 will not indicate a read-only status and TEST.3 will be a read-only file. An R is displayed to the left of read-only filenames. Figure 6.3 shows you what the screen should look similar to at this point in the exercise.

2. If you are not certain about the syntax of a DOS command, you can get help by entering the command name with the /? option. Use this option with several of the external commands discussed in this chapter (for example, **ATTRIB /?**).

3. To give a disk on Drive A a volume label, enter **LABEL A:** and follow the system prompts to enter a label of up to 11 characters (i.e., DATADISK). Enter **VOL A:** to verify the new volume label. Does your DOS disk have a volume label? Use the VOL command to check, but don't try to change it.

4. To hide all the files on Drive A that have a filename of TEST, enter **ATTRIB +H A:TEST.***. To display a directory listing of Drive A without including these hidden files enter **DIR A:**. Now enter the same command with the **/AH** option to display only the hidden files. Enter **ATTRIB -H A:TEST.*** to reset the hidden attribute so these files will normally be included in directory listings.

5. Enter **CHKDSK** to get a status report of the default drive (C:). Then enter **CHKDSK A:*.*** to get a status report of your data disk, directing the system to check for any fragmented files. Figure 6.4 shows the display screen after running CHKDSK. Your display screen should look similar to this one.

6. Delete all the TEST files on Drive A. Enter **UNDELETE A:/LIST** to see what files were deleted on Drive A. Your screen should look something like Figure 6.5. Then, enter **UNDELETE A:TEST.*** to restore them. Follow the instructions to undelete files and restore the first character of the filename (T). Finally, get a directory listing of Drive A to verify that the files were restored correctly.

7. Backing up hard disk files to floppy disks can be time-consuming. But backing up just the essential files is much better than no backup at all. Often this process requires many floppy disks. Use the following set of commands as many times as required, substituting a desired subdirectory name (i.e., C:\DOS) for "xxxxxx" to back up all files on that subdirectory to Drive A.

ATTRIB +A xxxxxx   (sets the archive attribute ON for all files)

XCOPY xxxxxx A: /M (copies all files with archive attribute ON, turning off each file attribute as it copies)

8. Bonus exercise (requires application of prior learning):

- Copy A:TEST.1 to A:TEST.ROF. Set the new file to read-only status and try to delete it. Then, reset the read-only attribute to allow writing to the file. Set the hidden file attribute of A:TEST.ROF to make it a hidden file and use the DIR command to verify that it is hidden. Before you continue, do whatever is required to delete A:TEST.ROF, and then restore it with the UNDELETE command.

- Use the LABEL command to eliminate the volume label on your data disk. Use the VOL command to confirm that it is no longer there. Then change it back to its previous value. Use the DIR command to confirm the change. This demonstrates that there are at least three commands that display a disk's volume label. What is another DOS command that displays the label?

This concludes the Chapter 6 hard disk lab exercises. When you are finished, remove your data disk.

HARD DISK MANAGEMENT

WORKING WITH SUBDIRECTORIES

HARD DISK COMMANDS

    CD (Change Directory) Command

    MD (Make Directory) Command

    RD (Remove Directory) Command

    PATH (Set Search Path) Command

    PROMPT (Set System Prompt) Command

    TREE (Display Tree) Command

    BACKUP Command

    RESTORE Command

HARD DISK MANAGEMENT TECHNIQUES

The management of files on hard disks is different from that of floppy disks. Floppy disks files are organized manually by grouping files on a disk and identifying each disk with a label. Hard disks are organized "electronically" into subdirectories, which provide a great advantage in working with the larger amount of data on hard disks.

This chapter teaches you how to work with subdirectories using commands primarily related to hard disks. The sample hierarchy of subdirectories (Figure 7.1) will be used extensively in this chapter. In addition, the term *directory* will often be used in place of the term subdirectory; a *subdirectory* is simply a lower-level directory.

Figure 7.1

**Sample Hierarchy of
Subdirectories**

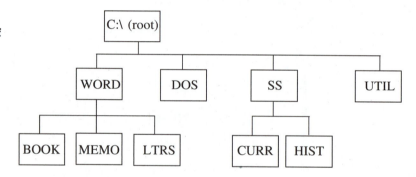

WORKING WITH SUBDIRECTORIES

DOS uses a preceding backslash (\) before a directory name to represent the break between one level in the hierarchy and the next level. Thus, the file BOSS.DOC stored in the MEMO directory is identified with the full filename C:\WORD\MEMO\BOSS.DOC. The full filename identifies the **path** of directories that must be taken by DOS to find the file in the hierarchy. If the path is not included in the filename, DOS looks for the file on the current directory. The **current (or default) directory** is the directory you are currently using. DOS treats the current directory as the default path, similar to the default disk concept. Commands entered from a specific directory use that directory as the default, unless otherwise noted. Here are some examples with C:\DOS as the current directory:

```
C:\DOS>DIR
```
(displays just the files in the DOS directory)

```
C:\DOS>CHKDSK *.*
```
(checks for file fragmentation in the DOS directory only)

```
C:\DOS>CHKDSK \*.*
```
(checks for file fragmentation in the root directory of Drive C)

A backslash at the beginning of the path tells DOS to begin looking for the directory from the root. If the backslash is not included, DOS starts looking from the current directory. If the file you need is not in the current directory, you must provide DOS the path to find it. The path is part of the full filename, as is the disk designator when a file is not on the default drive (see page 36).

It is advantageous to set up directories so that program files are separate from data files. Users can back up the directories containing data files (which change often) without having to back up program files (which do not change often). Directories containing program files need to be backed up only once, unless programs are added or modified.

DOS has several commands that let you create and use directories. You can change to another directory at any time from the system prompt. Directories on hard disks can have up to 512 entries, where an entry is a filename or directory name. When you use the DIR command, directories are identified with the symbol <DIR>. Because directory names do not have extensions, the command **DIR *.** displays all the directories in the current directory. Directory listings have a "dot" and a "double-dot" directory entry, sometimes called directory markers, like this:

```
.    <DIR> 8-15-92      9:45a
..   <DIR> 8-15-92      9:45a
```

The single dot represents the current directory and the double dot represents the **parent directory**, one level up from the current directory. Although the single dot is not used often, it can be used in place of "*.*". For example, the command **COPY . B:** copies all files from the current directory to Drive B. The double dot is used as shorthand notation to reference a parent directory. For example, if you are at the SS\HIST directory, the command **CD..** changes to the SS directory.

The following suggestions may prevent disk management problems when setting up your hard disk directory structure:

- Do not store any unnecessary programs or data files in the root directory. In most cases, only five files need to be in the root directory: the two hidden system files, COMMAND.COM, AUTOEXEC.BAT, and CONFIG.SYS.

- Do not assign extensions to your *directory* names.

- Do not give your directories long or confusing names. Although directory names can be 8 characters long, give them short and meaningful names like: DOS, UTIL, WP, DB, SS, and so on.

- Do not create directories more than two levels below the root directory.

HARD DISK COMMANDS

This chapter covers commands often used with hard disk systems, along with examples of usage. The following commands are introduced in a logical sequence to facilitate understanding.

CD — (Change Directory); Changes to another directory.

MD — (Make Directory); Creates a directory.

RD — (Remove Directory); Deletes a directory.

PATH — Instructs DOS where to look for command files.

PROMPT — Changes the system prompt.

TREE — Displays the complete directory tree structure.

BACKUP — Copies hard disk files to floppy disks.

RESTORE — Restores hard disk files from floppy disks.

Note: Commands marked with an asterisk (*) above can be executed using the DOS shell. The format for all commands designated as external (below) includes the optional parameters [d:][path] just before the command. These parameters designate the disk drive and the directory path DOS needs to find the external command.

CD (Change Directory) Command (internal) — also CHDIR

Syntax: `CD [d:][path]`

The **CD** command lets you change from the current directory to another one. The path is used to identify the directory you want to change to. For example, if you want to change to the root directory, you enter CD\. A leading backslash (\) in the path directs DOS to start the search path at the root directory. Normally, you want to start at the root directory to make sure DOS can find the directory. Entering the CD command with no parameters displays the current directory.

You can save keystrokes by recognizing that the symbols \ and . . are considered delimiters in DOS commands, just like a space and a slash (/). Thus, the commands CD\ and CD \ are the same.

Examples of usage:

```
C:\DOS> CD \
```
(changes to the root directory)

```
C:\DOS> Cd
```
(displays the current directory)

```
C:\DOS> cd\word\memo
```
(changes to the directory named MEMO on the WORD directory, starting from the root directory)

```
C:\> CD WORD\MEMO
```
(changes to the directory MEMO on the WORD directory, starting from the current directory)

```
C:\DOS> cd..
```
(changes to the parent directory)

Using the DOS Shell to Change Directories

To change to a different directory, just select the new directory in the Directory Tree. When you start the shell, only the first-level directories are displayed. A plus (+) sign next to a directory name indicates that the directory contains one or more subdirectories. If a subdirectory you want to change to is not included in the tree listing, you can expand the directory listings as follows:

KEYBOARD: Select the directory you want to expand and press the plus (+) key.

MOUSE: Click on the plus (+) sign next to the name of the appropriate directory.

To view *all directory levels* on the current disk, choose the **Expand All** option from the **Tree** pull-down menu. When a directory is expanded, a minus sign (–) displays next to the directory name. To collapse a directory, you can use the same process for expanding with one exception: use a minus sign in place of a plus sign.

MD (Make Directory) Command (internal) — also MKDIR

Syntax: `MD [d:]path`

The **MD** command creates a directory in a given location. You may create as many directories as you want, but keep in mind that too many directories can cause confusion. Directory names must be unique within a directory.

Examples of usage:

`C:\DOS> MD\word`
(creates a directory named WORD one level down from the root directory, as shown in Figure 7.1)

`C:\DOS> md \word\MEMO`
(creates a directory MEMO one level down from the directory named WORD, as shown in Figure 7.1)

`C:\> Md games`
(creates a directory called GAMES one level down from the current directory, which is the root directory in this example)

Using the DOS Shell to Create Directories

To simplify the process of creating a subdirectory, it is best if you select the parent directory as the current directory first. Then choose the **Create Directory** option from the **File** pull-down menu. After entering the subdirectory name in the text box, press the Enter key (or click on the OK command button) to create the new directory.

RD (Remove Directory) Command (internal) — also RMDIR

Syntax: `RD [d:]path`

The **RD** command removes a directory from a disk. *Before you can remove a directory it must be empty* (no files or subdirectories). DOS will remove the directory markers (the . and .. directories) automatically. You must change to another directory before removing the current directory. You can never remove the root directory.

Examples of usage:

`C:\DOS> rd \word\memo`
(removes the directory named MEMO from the WORD directory)

`C:\WORD> rd memo`
(removes directory MEMO from the current directory, WORD)

`C:\> RD\WORD`
(removes directory WORD from the root directory)

Using the DOS Shell to Remove Directories

The DOS shell has a nice feature not available from the command line. If you wish to remove a directory that is empty, select the directory (using the keyboard or mouse) and press the Del key. If it is empty, DOS will ask you to confirm that you wish to delete the selected directory. Press Y (or select Yes) to remove the directory.

PATH (Set Search Path) Command (internal)

Syntax: `PATH [d:][path][;path][;path]`

When you enter a command that is not an internal command, DOS searches the current directory (or the one specified in the command) for it. The **PATH** command directs DOS to search one or more directories for commands not found in the current directory. With a tree-structured directory, you cannot always access any command just by entering the command name. If it resides on a directory other than the current directory, you must specify the path so DOS can find it. The PATH command instructs DOS what directories to search, and in what order, to find a command that is not on the current directory. PATH only locates executable files, those with an extension of COM, EXE, or BAT. In each directory, DOS always looks for a matching command with a COM extension first. If it does not find one, it searches for an EXE extension, and finally a BAT extension. Whenever DOS cannot find the command to execute, it displays the message, "Bad command or filename."

The following important points relate to the PATH command:

• The search path is created with the PATH command.

• You may only have one search path active at a time.

• Directories are searched in the order of the search path.

- Typing mistakes in the path are not flagged as errors.
- Typing PATH with no parameters displays the current path.
- Entering PATH with just a semicolon tells the system you do not want any search path.
- Issuing a PATH command does not change the current directory.
- The length of the search path is limited to 127 characters.

Examples of usage:

`C:\DOS> Path \DOS`
(directs the system to look in the directory named DOS, if it cannot find a command in the current directory)

`C:\DOS> PATH \WORD\LTRS`
(directs DOS to look in LTRS within WORD to find a command, if it is not in the current directory)

`C:\DOS> path`
(displays the current search path setting)

`C:\DOS> Path ;`
(deletes the current search path setting)

`C:\DOS> PATH \;\UTIL;\DOS`
(directs DOS to search three directories in the order given: root, \UTIL, and \DOS)

PROMPT (Set System Prompt) Command (internal)

Syntax: `PROMPT [text]`
where text is a variable-length string of characters. Text may contain special codes in the form of $c, where c represents one of the following:

- **t** — the system time
- **d** — the system date
- **n** — the default (current) drive
- **g** — the > character
- **_** — the "new line" command (to skip a line)
- **p** — the default disk and current directory
- **e** — sends an escape code (used in Chapter 10)

The **PROMPT** command changes the appearance of the system prompt from the default (A> or C>) to a user-defined prompt. Placing a PROMPT command in your AUTOEXEC.BAT file changes the prompt automatically each time you boot. If you enter PROMPT with no text, DOS goes back to the default prompt. The special codes may be entered using either uppercase or lowercase.

It is very helpful to know where you are on a hard disk as you switch from one directory to the next. By using the $p code, the system prompt can be changed to display the current directory. For example, the command **PROMPT PG,** will display as **C:\DOS>** when the current directory is \DOS on Drive C. Figure 7.2 shows the results of executing the four PROMPT commands shown in Examples of Usage below.

Figure 7.2

Screen Display of Changing Prompts

```
C>PROMPT  Command?

Command?prompt  DATE = $d

DATE = Mon 07-27-1992prompt  Hi Fred $_$p$g

Hi Fred
C:\DOS>PROMPT

C>
```

Examples of Usage:

    C> PROMPT Command?
(changes the system prompt from C> to Command?)

    C> prompt DATE = $d
(changes system prompt to display DATE = followed by the system date)

    C> prompt Hi Fred $_$p$g
(displays Hi Fred on the first system prompt line followed by C> on the second line)

    C> PROMPT
(returns to the default system prompt)

TREE (Display Tree) Command (external)

Syntax: `[d:][path]TREE [d:][path] [/F] [/A]`

The **TREE** command displays all the directory paths on the specified drive. The first [d:][path] in the syntax of any external command is the path DOS needs to find it. The second [d:][path] lets you specify a disk and a directory, rather than displaying the tree structure for the current directory.

When the **/F** option is used, TREE lists all the files in the root directory and all directories on the disk. The **/A** option is used to send text characters whenever you have a printer that does not support graphic characters. Figure 7.3 shows a graphic display of a subdirectory structure.

Figure 7.3

Screen Display of Tree Structure Using TREE

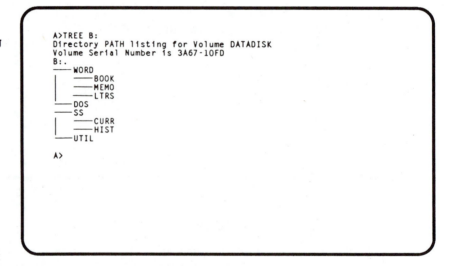

```
A>TREE B:
Directory PATH listing for Volume DATADISK
Volume Serial Number is 3A67-10FD
B:.
———— WORD
|      ————BOOK
|      ————MEMO
|      ————LTRS
————DOS
————SS
|      ————CURR
|      ————HIST
————UTIL

A>
```

When you are using the DOS shell, the directory tree is an integral part of the shell. A graphical tree structure is always displayed in the Directory Tree area. But the shell is limited; it cannot be used to print out the tree structure as you can with the TREE command.

Examples of usage:

`C:\DOS> TREE /F`
(displays all the files and directories in the current directory, which is the DOS directory on Drive C)

```
C:\DOS> TREE \WORD /F
```
(displays all files and directories in C:\WORD)

```
C:\> TREE >PRN
```
(prints a listing of all directories on Drive C)

```
C:\> tree /a >prn
```
(prints a listing of directories using text characters, rather than graphic characters)

BACKUP Command (external)

Syntax: `[d:][path]BACKUP [d]:[path][filename[.ext]] d:[/S][/M]`

where the first drive designator after the command is the source drive and the second designator is the target (output) drive.

The **BACKUP** command copies your hard disk files to as many formatted floppy disks as are needed to hold it in a compressed form. BACKUP automatically formats new disks, if required. You may include a full filename to restrict the files you want to back up. Wildcard characters may be used in the file name.

BACKUP has two options that make it easier to back up your files. The command BACKUP C: A: will back up only the files in the root directory of Drive C to a disk in Drive A. You can use the **/S** option to copy all lower-level subdirectory files, in addition to the files in a directory. Thus, to back up all files, add the /S option to this command. The **/M** option uses the archive attribute to back up only those files modified since the last backup.

Whenever BACKUP fills a floppy disk, DOS prompts you to insert a new disk. Label each backup disk in consecutive order so you can restore them in the same order.

Note: *BACKUP is not the same as COPY*. When files are recorded on a backup disk with BACKUP, they cannot be used until they are restored to the hard disk with the RESTORE command.

Examples of usage:

```
C:\DOS> BACKUP C:\*.* A:/S
```
(backs up all files in all directories of Drive C to Drive A)

```
C:\DOS> backup c:\word\book\*.doc a:/m
```
(backs up only files in the BOOK directory within WORD that have an extension of DOC and have been modified since the last backup on that directory)

```
C:\DOS> Backup C:\*.txt a: /s
```
(backs up all files with an extension of TXT from all directories on the hard disk)

Using the DOS Shell to Back Up and Restore Hard Disks

To back up a fixed disk, choose the **Backup Fixed Disk** program from the **Disk Utilities** list in the Main program menu area. If you have a hard disk, the default parameters and options in the accompanying text box are identical to the first example of usage above. Just press the Enter key to back up all files in all directories of the hard disk to Drive A. Other parameters and options that can be used are the same as with the system prompt. To restore files to a hard disk with the shell, choose the **Restore Fixed Disk** option from the **Disk Utilities** list. The RESTORE command is covered next.

RESTORE Command (external)

Syntax: `[d:][path]RESTORE d: [d:][path]filename [.ext] [/S] [/P]`

where the first drive designator after the command is the source drive (with the backup files) and the second is the target drive.

The **RESTORE** command restores one or more files from backup disks created with the BACKUP command. RESTORE can recreate files backed up using BACKUP from any previous version of DOS. An optional filename parameter lets you specify which files to restore. Wildcard characters may be used for the full filename with the RESTORE command. When multiple backup disks are involved, DOS prompts you to insert the next disk.

The **/S** option lets you restore deleted directories on a hard disk, if needed. For example: prior to having your hard disk repaired, assume you saved your files with BACKUP to Drive A. Further assume that during the repair process, all of your hard disk files were destroyed. You could enter **RESTORE C: A:*.* /S** to restore all the subdirectories and files on the backup disk to the repaired hard disk.

The **/P** option directs DOS to pause before restoring certain files. In addition to restoring specified files, it prompts you for permission to restore files that are read-only, or that have changed since the last backup. Changed files will have the archive attribute set ON. It lets you confirm with a Y or N response whether you want to restore that file.

Examples of usage:

```
C:\DOS> RESTORE A: C:\SS\*.*
```
(restores all files in the SS directory from the backup disks)

```
C:\DOS> restore a: c:\*.doc /s
```
(restores all files with an extension of DOC for all directories)

```
C:\> RESTORE B: C:\*.* /S/P
```
(prompts you before restoring each file with the archive or read-only attribute ON in Drive C, using backup file data from Drive B)

HARD DISK MANAGEMENT TECHNIQUES

One of the most difficult areas of DOS to master is effective control and management of all the files that accumulate on hard disks. Several techniques for managing hard disks have already been discussed. Figure 7.4 provides a good overview of hard disk management techniques.

Chapter 7

Review Questions

1. How are files organized on hard disks?
2. What is the significance of the term "current directory" in DOS?
3. How are subdirectory names identified by DOS?
4. What is a DOS path?
5. Why might you want to have relatively short subdirectory names?
6. What do the single-dot and double-dot directory entries represent in DOS?
7. What command switches from the current directory to another directory?
8. How do you switch to the root directory?
9. Describe how a specific directory in the Directory Tree area of the DOS shell is expanded using a mouse.
10. How can identical filenames (i.e., FORMAT.COM) exist multiple times on the same hard disk?
11. What specific command creates a directory named DOS under the root directory if the current subdirectory is \UTIL?

Figure 7.4

Hard Disk Management Techniques

- Develop good file naming conventions to help you better organize files.
- Use standard filename extensions to aid in classifying file types.
- Make backup copies of important data files regularly.
- Organize hard disk files into logical tree subdirectories.
- Place data files on a separate subdirectory from program files. This will shorten the time it takes to back up only your data files. Program files do not need to be backed up on a regular basis.
- Use AUTOEXEC.BAT and CONFIG.SYS files to customize your boot process.
- Limit your root directory files to only those used for booting, such as the COMMAND.COM, CONFIG.SYS, and AUTOEXEC.BAT files.
- Use PROMPT PG in an AUTOEXEC.BAT file to change the system prompt to display the current directory location.
- Use the PATH command in an AUTOEXEC.BAT file to tell DOS where to look to find program files that are not on the current directory.
- Regularly issue the DIR command to verify which files are on the current directory.
- Use DIR*. to display directory names in the current directory. Directory names do not have extensions.
- Use CD.. to change to the parent directory in the tree, one up from the current directory.
- Periodically use CHKDSK *.* /F to identify file fragmentation and fix any lost allocation clusters on the disk.
- Use a utility program to eliminate file fragmentation from your hard disk.
- Delete any unnecessary backup (BAK) and temporary (TMP) files on your hard disk.
- If you have only one floppy drive, create a temporary directory on hard disk to serve as a transfer area for copying files from one floppy disk to another.
- Always park the read/write heads of your hard disk before you turn off your computer, especially before you attempt to move it.
- Use a backup power supply to ensure a good supply of power to your computer. This will minimize any physical damage to your hard disk and/or loss of data.

12. What specific command creates a directory named DOS under the current directory?

13. How do you remove a directory from a disk?

14. How are multiple directories specified in the PATH command?

15. When multiple directories are included in a search path, which one is searched first?

16. What command is used to view the current search path?

17. What command displays only directory names in the root directory?

18. What command is used to display all directory names and their files on a disk?

19. What kinds of files may be restored with the RESTORE command?

20. How can directories be restored?

Chapter 7

Floppy Disk Lab Exercises

Most of the following exercises can be executed within the DOS shell. Your instructor can decide which approach (the shell or command line) should be used to complete these exercises.

1. Make a hierarchy of directories on Drive B according to Figure 7.1 as shown below.

   A> MD B:\DOS
   A> MD B:\UTIL
   A> MD B:\WORD
   A> MD B:\WORD\BOOK
   A> MD B:\WORD\MEMO
   A> MD B:\WORD\LTRS
   A> MD B:\SS
   A> MD B:\SS\CURR
   A> MD B:\SS\HIST

2. Copy a file currently residing in the root directory of Drive B to each of the nine directories created in Exercise 1 above. For example:

   COPY B:READ.ME B:\WORD

3. Check out your new directory structure by entering:

   A> DIR B: (lists files and directories in root directory)
   A> DIR B:\WORD (lists all files and directories in \WORD — the screen should look similar to Figure 7.5)
   A> TREE B:/F (lists all files and directories on Drive B — the hierarchy of directories should look similar to Figure 7.6)

4. Work in different directories:

   A> B: (change default drive to B)
   B> CD\WORD\MEMO (make MEMO the current directory)
   B> DIR (test change to desired directory only)
   B> CD (change back to root directory)
   B> DIR (list all files and directories on the root directory of the default drive)

Figure 7.5

Screen Display of Directories in \WORD

```
B:\>DIR B:\WORD

 Volume in drive B is DATADISK
 Volume Serial Number is 3A67-10FD
 Directory of B:\WORD

 .            <DIR>        07-27-92  10:55a
 ..           <DIR>        07-27-92  10:55a
 BOOK         <DIR>        07-27-92  10:55a
 MEMO         <DIR>        07-27-92  10:55a
 LTRS         <DIR>        07-27-92  10:55a
 READ     ME          223 07-27-92  10:24a
          6 file(s)          223 bytes
                         586752 bytes free

B:\>
```

5. Delete the directory named HIST:

B> DEL \SS\HIST*.* (enter Y to delete all files from HIST)
B> RD \SS\HIST (remove HIST directory)
B> A:TREE B: (test the removal of HIST by running TREE, which is an external command on Drive A)

6. Set up a path to your DOS external commands:

B> PATH A: (set path to include Drive A)
B> TREE B: (test the path, noting that it will find TREE on Drive A after first searching Drive B)

7. Change the system prompt to display the current directory. Then change to several directories to see the effect:

B> PROMPT PG
B> CD\WORD
B> CD\SS\CURR
B> CD..
B> CD

8. Bonus exercise (requires application of prior learning):

• Change the default disk to Drive B. Copy all the TEST files from the root directory of Drive B to the DOS directory on Drive B, created previously in this lab exercise.

• From the root directory of Drive B, create directory TEMP.

• Change to TEMP, copy all TEST files from B:\DOS to TEMP, and use the DIR command to verify the copy process. Use

Figure 7.6
TREE Structure of Drive B

```
A>Directory PATH listing for Volume DATADISK
Volume Serial Number is 3A67-10FD
B:.
    COMMAND.COM
    READ.ME
    TEST.1
    TEST.3
    TEST.4
    TEST.ROF

├──DOS
        READ.ME

├──UTIL
        READ.ME

├──WORD
        READ.ME

    ├──BOOK
        READ.ME

    ├──MEMO
        READ.ME

    └──LTRS
        READ.ME

└──SS
        READ.ME

    ├──CURR
        READ.ME

    └──HIST
        READ.ME
```

wildcard characters whenever possible to save keystrokes and minimize errors.

• Finally, remove the TEMP directory and change back to the A> prompt. Did you remember to delete all the files in TEMP first?

This ends the Chapter 7 floppy disk lab exercises. Remove your disk(s) when you are done.

Chapter 7

Hard Disk Lab Exercises

Most of the following exercises can be executed within the DOS shell. Your instructor can decide which approach (the shell or command line) should be used to complete these exercises.

1. Make a hierarchy of directories on Drive A according to Figure 7.1 as shown below.

   C:\DOS> MD A:\DOS
   C:\DOS> MD A:\UTIL
   C:\DOS> MD A:\WORD
   C:\DOS> MD A:\WORD\BOOK
   C:\DOS> MD A:\WORD\MEMO
   C:\DOS> MD A:\WORD\LTRS
   C:\DOS> MD A:\SS
   C:\DOS> MD A:\SS\CURR
   C:\DOS> MD A:\SS\HIST

2. Copy a file currently residing in the root directory of Drive A to each of the nine directories created above. For example:

   COPY A:READ.ME A:\WORD

3. Check out your new directory structure by entering:

   C:\DOS> DIR A: (lists files and directories in root directory)
   C:\DOS> DIR A:\WORD (lists all files and directories in \WORD — the screen should look similar to Figure 7.5)
   C:\DOS> TREE A:/F (lists all files and directories on Drive A — the hierarchy of directories should look similar to Figure 7.6)

4. Work in different directories:

   C:\DOS> A: (change default drive to A)
   A> CD\WORD\MEMO (make MEMO the current directory)
   A> DIR (test change to desired directory only)
   A> CD (change back to root directory)
   A> DIR (list all files and directories on the root directory of the default drive)

5. Delete the directory named HIST:

A> DEL \SS\HIST*.* (enter Y to delete all files from HIST)
A> RD \SS\HIST (remove HIST directory)
A> C:\DOS\TREE A: (test the removal of HIST by running TREE, which is an external command on Drive C)

6. Set up a path to your DOS external commands:

A> PATH C:\DOS (set path to include the DOS directory on Drive C)
A> TREE (test the path, noting that it will find TREE on Drive C after first searching Drive A)

7. Change the system prompt to display the current directory. Then change to several directories to see the effect:

A> PROMPT PG
A> CD\WORD
A> CD\SS\CURR
A> CD..
A> CD

8. Bonus exercise (requires application of prior learning):

- Change the default disk to Drive A. Copy all the TEST files from the root directory of Drive A to the DOS directory on Drive A, created previously in this lab exercise.

- From the root directory of Drive A, create directory TEMP.

- Change to TEMP, copy all TEST files from A:\DOS to TEMP, and use the DIR command to verify the copy process. Use wildcard characters whenever possible to save keystrokes and minimize errors.

- Finally, remove the TEMP directory and change back to the C:\DOS> prompt. Did you remember to delete all the files in TEMP first?

This ends the Chapter 7 hard disk lab exercises. Remove your data disk when you are done.

THREE IMPORTANT CONCEPTS

REDIRECTION

PIPING WITH FILTERS

> **SORT Command**
>
> **MORE Command**
>
> **FIND Command**

COMMAND LINE EDITING

> **DOS Editing Keys**
>
> **DOSKEY Command**

Chapter 8

THREE IMPORTANT CONCEPTS

This chapter presents three DOS concepts that will be very helpful to you. The first concept is the use of redirection. It is a technique used for changing the standard input or output device of a DOS command, thereby adding flexibility to your commands. Closely related to redirection is piping, a method of transferring the output of one command as input to another. It lets you combine DOS commands on a single command line. Special-purpose commands known as filters are used with redirection and piping. Filters modify portions of the information that passes through them. DOS has three filters: SORT, MORE, and FIND. The last important concept, command line editing, lets you make changes to a previous DOS command without having to retype it.

REDIRECTION

Redirection changes the standard output device used by a DOS command to another output device. It can also redirect the standard input device. The standard input device is the keyboard and the standard output device is the display screen. The "less than" sign (<) defines a new source of input and the "greater than" sign (>) defines a new target of output. In the examples that follow, the first > is part of the system prompt (i.e., A>).

Examples of usage:

```
A> DIR  >  B:DIR.LST
```
(redirects the standard output display of the DIR command from the screen to a file on Drive B named DIR.LST)

```
A> dir  >  prn
```
(directs the DIR display to go to the printer)

```
A> CHKDSK >PRN
```
(redirects the displayed output to the printer)

```
A> Sort  <  B:filea.txt  >  B:fileb.txt
```
(Use FILEA.TXT as the input for a SORT command, or filter, that redirects the sorted results to FILEB.TXT)

PIPING WITH FILTERS

Piping uses the output from one DOS command as the input for another DOS command. DOS transfers (pipes) data by creating a temporary work file on the default disk. Thus, the default disk cannot be full or write-protected. The first command outputs to a piping file, which is used as input by the second command. Multiple piping files are created if required. When the final operation is completed, DOS deletes all temporary pipe files. You can think of piping as a form of redirection. With piping, however, the temporary files are created and deleted by DOS rather than by the user.

Piping usually involves DOS commands called filters. **Filters** accept data, do something with it, and pass it to the next step. The DOS commands most often used with piping are:

SORT — Sorts an ASCII file into a desired sequence.

MORE — Displays only one screen of output at a time, pausing to let the user press any key to continue.

FIND — Searches a file for a specified string of text.

Because filters are external DOS commands, a disk drive designator is required if they are not on the default disk. The symbol used by DOS to define a piping operation is the broken vertical bar (¦) located on top of the \ key. The standard output device for the TYPE and SORT commands is the monitor. If you pipe the output from TYPE into a SORT command, the monitor displays the sorted listing of the file in ascending sequence. For example:

```
A> TYPE  PHONE.LST  ¦ SORT
```

If your PHONE.LST contained names of friends with their phone numbers, this command would display them in name sequence. The above example is equivalent to the following set of commands:

```
TYPE  PHONE.LST  >  A:TEMPFILE
SORT  <  A:TEMPFILE
DEL  A:TEMPFILE
```

SORT Command (external)

SORT arranges data according to an industry standard using each character's ASCII value. The default sequence places lines of data in ascending order as follows:

1. Spaces come first.

2. Most of the special characters come next.

3. Numeric characters (0–9) are sequenced next.

4. Uppercase alphabetic characters come next.

5. Lowercase alphabetic characters are last.

To reverse the order of a sort, include the reverse option (**/R**). The following command produces a listing in descending order:

```
A> TYPE   PHONE.LST   ¦ SORT  /R
```

MORE Command (external)

If you find that a sorted listing is too large to fit on a single screen, you can pipe it to the **MORE** command. Figure 8.1 shows what the first page might look like when the following is executed:

```
A> TYPE   PHONE.LST   ¦ SORT  ¦ MORE
```

Figure 8.1

Screen Display of Sorted PHONE.LST

```
ALLISON, EDWARD          634-1114
ALLISON, JERRY           635-7711
ALLISON, JIM             634-0055
ALLISON, MOLLY           634-0111
ALLISON, SUSAN           634-2341
ANDERSON, ANNA           634-6003
ANDERSON, DAVID          635-0089
ANDERSON, HARRY          634-0123
ANDERSON, SUSAN          634-7539
ANDERSON, WALLY          635-9016
ATWATER, KELLY           635-9962
BAKER, RICHARD           635-8009
FRANKLIN, BENJAMIN       635-6388
FRANKLIN, EDWARD         635-8902
FRANKLIN, FRANCES        635-9154
FRANKLIN, PENNY          635-2284
GAPEN, ANN               635-8442
JENSON, JOSEPH           634-2276
JENSON, SUZI             635-9022
SAMPSON, DAVID           634-7861
SAMPSON, SUSAN           635-8873
WATSON, EDWARD           635-4567
-- More --
```

FIND Command (external)

The **FIND** command searches files for a given string of characters. It locates all lines from the specified file(s) that contain the desired characters. The text entered must be enclosed in a set of double quote marks and must use the correct uppercase and lowercase. For example, suppose PHONE.LST contained uppercase names and phone numbers. To display the phone number for everyone named Susan, enter:

```
A> TYPE   PHONE.LST   ¦ FIND   "SUSAN"
```

However, FIND would not locate any files in the following example because PHONE.LST only contains uppercase characters.

```
C> TYPE   PHONE.LST   ¦ FIND   "Susan"
```

Figure 8.2 shows what the screen might look like after the last two TYPE and FIND commands were executed.

Figure 8.2

Screen Display of FIND

```
A>TYPE PHONE.LST ¦ FIND "SUSAN"
ALLISON, SUSAN          634-2341
ANDERSON, SUSAN         634-7539
WILSON, SUSAN           635-7921
WATSON, SUSAN           634-5530
SAMPSON, SUSAN          635-8873

A>TYPE PHONE.LST ¦ FIND "Susan"

A>
```

The FIND command can be used with any file or ASCII listing, such as the output of a DIR listing. To display a directory of just the files that were created (or changed) on November 16, 1992, enter the following command:

```
A> DIR ¦ FIND  "11-16-92"
```

Using filters can give you the ability to create your own commands. For example, suppose you wanted to display all the files on Drive C with an extension of BAK, one screen at a time. You could "create" your own new command as follows:

```
C:\DOS> CHKDSK /V ¦ FIND ".BAK"  ¦ MORE
```

Piping and redirection may be combined in a single operation. To have a sorted directory listing saved to an ASCII file called B:SORTED.TXT, you could enter the following:

```
A> DIR ¦ SORT  >  B:SORTED.TXT
```

Sometimes it is useful to display data from a listable file on the screen, one screen at a time. If ACCOUNT.TXT was a large file on Drive B, you could enter:

```
A> MORE  <  B:ACCOUNT.TXT
```

This directs MORE to get its input from B:ACCOUNT.TXT. MORE displays its output on the monitor one screen at a time. You could have obtained the same result with piping by entering:

```
A> TYPE  B:ACCOUNT.TXT  ¦ MORE
```

In this case, redirection is more efficient than piping because it does not have to create and delete a temporary piping file.

COMMAND LINE EDITING

There will be times you want to execute a previous DOS command, exactly as you entered it earlier, or with some minor change. DOS keeps track of the commands you enter, letting you recall them on a selective basis. Once recalled, you can change the command before pressing the Enter key to execute it. DOS supports this process, called **command line editing,** in two ways: with DOS editing keys, and with the DOSKEY command.

DOS Editing Keys

Sometimes you need to make minor changes to the last DOS command entered. Rather than rekeying the entire command line, you can use the **DOS editing keys** to recall it and change only the characters that need changing.

When you enter a command, DOS puts a copy of it in a temporary storage location called an input buffer. You can recall the last command from the buffer and make changes without duplicating keystrokes. The process of editing involves inserting and deleting characters in the command line. Figure 8.3 is a summary of the DOS editing keys used most often.

Figure 8.3
DOS Editing Keys

<F1> — Displays one character at a time from the buffer.

<F3> — Displays all characters in the buffer (or the rest of the buffer).

<Ins> — Inserts one or more characters in the buffer at the cursor location.

<Del> — Deletes one character at a time from the buffer.

The best way to understand how to use the DOS editing keys is to try them. The three exercises that follow show you how to use the editing keys and will help reinforce what you have learned.

1. Suppose you entered **COPY A:TEST1.XT A:TEST1.BAK** and were given an error message because TEST1.XT was not found on Drive A (assume it should have been TEST1.TXT). To correct the command with the editing keys:

- Press **\<F1\>** until the X is next to be retrieved, displaying COPY A:TEST1.

- Press **\<INS\>** and the letter **T**.

- Press **\<F3\>** to display the rest of the buffer. Now it should show **COPY A:TEST1.TXT A:TEST1.BAK**.

- Press **Enter** to execute the command and get back to the system prompt. It is normal to get an error message at this point because the file TEST1.TXT does not exist on Drive A.

2. Suppose you entered **COPY A:TEST3.DOC A:TEST.BAK** and wanted to redo it because you meant to copy to A:TEST3.BAK. To correct the error:

- Press **\<F3\>** to display all characters in the input buffer.

- Use the **Backspace key** to delete the last four characters (.BAK).

- Type **3.BAK** and press **Enter**.

3. Suppose you entered **TYPE A:TEST3.DOC** and got what you wanted, but now you also want to display A:TEST2.DOC.

- Press **\<F1\>** until the 3 in the filename is the next to be displayed.

- Press **2** to replace the next character (the 3) in the buffer.

- Press **\<F3\>** to finish displaying the buffer and then press Enter.

DOSKEY Command (external)

The DOS editing keys can only recall and modify the last command entered. **DOSKEY** can recall and edit previously entered commands. It uses a special buffer area that saves the last 48 commands. However, DOSKEY must be executed before it can start saving commands. It is called a **Terminate-and-Stay-Resident (TSR)** program because it stays in RAM until you turn off the system or reboot DOS. To install DOSKEY, enter **DOSKEY** at the system prompt.

To work with a previous command from the buffer, use the Up arrow key to find the desired command. If you go back too far, use the Down arrow key to go forward. The Page Up and Page Down keys are used to recall the first and last commands in the buffer, respectively. For example, let us assume that you have just finished entering the following commands:

```
A> DOSKEY
A> DIR  B:
A> DBASE
A> COPY  B:TESTFILE.DOC  A:*.BAK
A> DIR A: /W
A>
```

To recall the COPY command to execute it again with minor changes, press the Up arrow key twice — once for the last command entered (DIR), and a second time to recall the COPY command. Editing keys can be used to make changes to the current command line. Figure 8.4 lists the DOSKEY editing keys and their functions within a command line.

Figure 8.4

DOSKEY Editing Keys

KEY	FUNCTION
Left arrow	Moves the cursor back one character.
Right arrow	Moves the cursor forward one character.
HOME key	Moves the cursor to the beginning of the command line.
END key	Moves the cursor to the end of the command line.
Ins key	Toggles the insert mode on or off.
Del key	Deletes the character at the location of the cursor.
Esc key	Cancels editing, leaving the command line unchanged.

Chapter 8

Review Questions

1. What is the standard input device in DOS?

2. What is the standard output device in DOS?

3. How would you use redirection to print a directory listing?

4. What is a "piping file" and how is it used?

5. What type of files are resequenced by the SORT command?

6. What does the /R option do when added to the SORT command?

7. What is the purpose of the MORE filter?

8. What is displayed with the command **DIR ¦ FIND "CONFIG"**?

9. What command displays A:README.TXT a screen at a time?

10. What two different commands may be entered to print the contents of A:README.TXT?

11. What command can be entered to view just the displayed number of files in a directory listing? *Hint*: Use a unique string of characters like "(s)".

12. What two methods are used to edit the DOS command line?

13. When are DOS editing keys used?

14. What DOS editing key displays all the characters in the buffer?

15. How are characters deleted from the input buffer of a command line?

16. What is the primary use for the DOSKEY command?

17. Assuming DOSKEY is installed and you have entered several DOS commands, where will the cursor be after you press the Up arrow key followed by the HOME key?

18. What will the command **CHKDSK /V ¦ SORT > PRN** accomplish?

19. Once you start changing a command line with the DOS editing keys, how can you abort the process and leave the command line unchanged?

20. Why does DOSKEY need to remain in RAM when executed?

Chapter 8

Floppy Disk Lab Exercises

These exercises should all be done from the system prompt.

1. For this exercise, you will be creating some temporary files on the DOS disk. Therefore, you should remove any write-protect tab on the DOS disk. Boot DOS (Drive A) and insert your data disk in Drive B. Enter **DIR B**: and experiment with redirection and piping as follows:

DIR > B:TEST1.DIR

(redirects the directory from the monitor to a file named TEST1.DIR)

SORT < B:TEST1.DIR > B:TEST2.DIR

(sorts the previous file and redirects it to another filename)

TYPE B:TEST2.DIR ¦ MORE

(displays the sorted directory listing)

DIR ¦ SORT > B:TEST3.DIR

(outputs the sorted directory to a file)

TYPE B:TEST3.DIR ¦ MORE

(displays a file, one screen at a time)

DIR /OS ¦ MORE

(lists the directory of the default disk ordered by file size)

DIR B:/O-S

(lists a directory of Drive B ordered by descending file size — the screen should look similar to Figure 8.5)

Figure 8.5

Screen Display of Sorted Directory

```
A>DIR B:/O-S

 Volume in drive B is DATADISK
 Volume Serial Number is 3A67-10FD
 Directory of B:\

COMMAND  COM     47845 04-09-91    5:00a
TEST3    DIR      1032 07-28-92    8:21a
TEST1    DIR       950 07-28-92    8:19a
TEST2    DIR       950 07-28-92    8:20a
READ     ME        223 07-27-92   10:24a
TEST     1         223 07-27-92   10:24a
TEST     3         223 07-27-92   10:24a
TEST     4         223 07-27-92   10:24a
TEST     ROF       223 07-27-92   10:24a
DOS           <DIR>       07-27-92   10:54a
UTIL          <DIR>       07-27-92   10:55a
WORD          <DIR>       07-27-92   10:55a
SS            <DIR>       07-27-92   10:55a
        13 file(s)      51892 bytes
                       580608 bytes free

A>
```

2. If you are connected to a printer, you can complete this portion of the lab exercise. Otherwise, just read it. To print a sorted directory listing by file size on the printer, rather than display it on the monitor, enter **DIR /OS > PRN.**

   To print a sorted directory of just those files on Drive B with a filename containing "TEST" on the printer, enter the following:

   ```
   DIR   B:  ¦ FIND   "TEST"   ¦ SORT  >  PRN
   ```

3. Install the DOSKEY command by entering DOSKEY at the system prompt. If DOSKEY cannot be installed, ask your instructor for help.

4. Experiment with DOS editing keys by entering the following:

   DIR A: (press Enter to execute this command)
   DIR A:/P (use F3 to allow you to easily add /P)
   COPY B:TEST3.DR B:TEST3.BAK (forces the message, File not found)
   COPY B:TEST3.DIR B:TEST3.BAK (use the Dos editing keys to correct the previous entry)

5. If DOSKEY is installed (see Exercise 3), recall the last few commands you entered by pressing the Up arrow key. You can scroll down through the list by using the Down arrow key. When you locate the command that resulted in a directory listing of Drive A with the pause option, add the /OE option to it and press the Enter key to get the directory in extension sequence.

6. Bonus exercise (requires application of prior learning):

- Enter **SORT < B:READ.ME > B:READ.SRT** to create a new file, the sorted equivalent of the READ.ME file on Drive B. Use the TYPE command to display it on the screen. Notice that complete lines of text were sorted (see Figure 8.6), not each word.

- Enter **TYPE B:READ.ME ¦ FIND "comma"** to display only those lines in the file containing the string "comma". Repeat this operation using "comma ". How did adding a space to the FIND string affect the output?

Figure 8.6
Screen Display of
READ.SRT

```
A>SORT <B:READ.ME >B:READ.SRT

A>TYPE B:READ.SRT
either a space or a comma.  They can be used interchangeably
must be separated by delimiters.  Delimiters are normally
When entering DOS commands, the commands and parameters
within any command (i.e., COPY A:OLDFILE,B:).

A>
```

This is the end of the Chapter 8 floppy disk lab exercises. Don't forget to remove your disk(s) when you are done.

Chapter 8
Hard Disk Lab Exercises

All of these exercises should be done from the system prompt.

1. Boot DOS (Drive C) and insert your data disk in Drive A. Make sure you are at the DOS portion of the hard disk before proceeding. Enter **DIR A:** and experiment with redirection and piping as follows:

DIR > A:TEST1.DIR

(redirects the directory from the monitor to a file named TEST1.DIR)

SORT < A:TEST1.DIR > A:TEST2.DIR

(sorts the previous file and redirects it to another filename)

TYPE A:TEST2.DIR ¦ MORE

(displays the sorted directory listing)

DIR ¦ SORT > A:TEST3.DIR

(outputs the sorted directory to a file)

TYPE A:TEST3.DIR ¦ MORE

(displays a file, one screen at a time)

DIR /OS ¦ MORE

(lists the directory of the default disk ordered by file size)

DIR A:/O-S

(lists a directory of Drive A ordered by descending file size — the screen should look similar to Figure 8.5)

2. If you are connected to a printer, you can complete this portion of the lab exercise. Otherwise, just read it. To print a sorted directory listing by file size on the printer, rather than display it on the monitor, enter **DIR /OS > PRN.**

   To print a sorted directory of just those filenames on Drive A with a filename containing "TEST" on the printer, enter the following:

   ```
   DIR   A:  ¦ FIND    "TEST"   ¦ SORT   >   PRN
   ```

3. Install the DOSKEY command by entering **DOSKEY** at the system prompt. If DOSKEY cannot be installed, ask your instructor for help.

4. Experiment with DOS editing keys by entering the following:

   DIR (press Enter to execute this command)
   DIR /P (use F3 to allow you to easily add /P)
   COPY A:TEST3.DR A:TEST3.BAK (forces the message, File not found)
   COPY A:TEST3.DIR A:TEST3.BAK (use the DOS editing keys to correct the previous entry)

5. If DOSKEY is installed (see Exercise 3), recall the last few commands you entered by pressing the Up arrow key. You can scroll down through the list by using the Down arrow key. When you locate the command that resulted in a directory listing with the pause option, add the /OE option to it and press the Enter key to get the directory in extension sequence.

6. Bonus exercise (requires application of prior learning):

- **Enter SORT < A:READ.ME > A:READ.SRT** to create a new file, the sorted equivalent of the READ.ME file on Drive A. Use the TYPE command to display it on the screen. Notice that complete lines of text were sorted (see Figure 8.6), not each word.

- **Enter TYPE A:READ.ME ¦ FIND "comma"** to display only those lines in the file containing the string "comma". Repeat this operation using "comma ". How did adding a space to the FIND string affect the output?

This is the end of the Chapter 8 hard disk lab exercises. Don't forget to remove your data disk when you are done.

INTRODUCTION TO BATCH FILES

Chapter 9

INTRODUCTION TO BATCH FILES

Thus far you have learned how to execute DOS commands by entering them one after another at the system prompt. A **batch file** is a group of commands that the computer automatically executes as a set, instead of one at a time. This text file, which must have an extension of BAT, contains an entire "batch" of commands. DOS's ability to create and run batch files is a powerful feature. All of its commands are executed in sequence without intervention, freeing you to do other things while the computer does all the work. The primary objectives of this chapter are for you:

- To understand how batch files work, including the AUTOEXEC.BAT file.

- To see how replaceable parameters can add flexibility to batch files.

- To learn how to use the REM, PAUSE, and ECHO batch file commands.

- To learn how the full-screen text editor (EDIT) can be used to create and modify batch files.

THE AUTOEXEC.BAT FILE

For any command to be executed whenever DOS starts, the command must be placed in a special batch file called **AUTOEXEC.BAT**, appropriately named for AUTOmatic EXECution. This is especially useful with hard disk systems that utilize the PROMPT and PATH commands. Other commands used during the boot process are covered later.

Immediately after DOS is booted, a ROM chip searches for an AUTOEXEC.BAT file on the root directory of the system disk. If one is found, DOS executes any commands contained in AUTOEXEC.BAT, bypassing the automatic prompting for DATE and TIME. If you do not have a battery-powered clock-calendar in your computer, you must include the DATE and TIME commands in your AUTOEXEC.BAT file. Otherwise, you can let DOS automatically set the system date and time from your clock-calendar. *If you have a hard disk system, you most likely have an AUTOEXEC.BAT file already — so don't change it or delete it accidentally.*

Suppose you were setting up an office accounting system that required a specific set of tasks to be done whenever the system was booted. You could use an AUTOEXEC.BAT file containing the specific commands you require. It could look similar to Figure 9.1.

Figure 9.1
Sample
AUTOEXEC.BAT File

```
PATH C:\DOS;C:\UTIL;C:\MENU
PROMPT $P$G
SET DIRCMD=/ON
COPY C:\SSFILES\BUDGET.WK1 A:BUDGET.BAK
CD C:\SS
LOTUS
```

The computer automatically executes these commands each time the system is turned on. This AUTOEXEC.BAT file assumes that the system date and time is automatically updated from a hardware clock-calendar. It executes the following tasks each time the system is booted:

- Sets the default search path to use C:\DOS, C:\UTIL, and C:\MENU.
- Causes the system prompt to display the current disk and directory.
- Sets the default for directory listings to be in filename sequence.
- Copies a file on the SSFILES directory of the hard disk to Drive A.
- Changes to the SS directory on the hard disk.
- Executes an application program called LOTUS.

This approach would simplify and standardize the startup procedures for any system. A batch file may be as simple or as complex as you want it to be. It keeps you from the tedious task of having to enter a group of commands each time. In addition, it lets you relax while the computer works for you.

CREATING BATCH FILES

Suppose you didn't want to enter CHKDSK every time you wanted DOS to check a disk. You could create a simple batch file called CK.BAT that lets you execute the CHKDSK command by entering **CK**, the batch file name. Whenever you enter the name of an external command, such as FORMAT or CHKDSK, DOS searches for it on the specified disk. If it is found, DOS executes the command. Executing a batch file works in much the same way. You must enter the batch file name to allow DOS to find and execute the batch file. When you enter a DOS command or a batch file command, the system looks for a command to execute in the current directory. It first looks for a COM file with that name. If a COM file is not found, DOS looks for an EXE file and then a BAT file. It is normally recommended that you give batch files names different from COM or EXE files. Otherwise, the DOS command with that name may be found and executed before the batch file is found.

Because you already know how to use the COPY CON command, use it to create a one-line batch file from the keyboard (CONsole) as shown below. Press the Enter key after each line is keyed. Always press the F6 function key <F6> and then the Enter key at the end of the last line of text to exit the COPY operation.

```
A> COPY CON CK.BAT <Enter>
CHKDSK <F6> <Enter>
```

From now on, when you want to execute CHKDSK, you only need to enter CK to execute this batch file. However, CK.BAT is only able to execute CHKDSK for Drive A (the default drive). What if you wanted run it for another drive?

USING REPLACEABLE PARAMETERS

Many DOS commands require parameters that vary each time you enter the command. Batch file features called **replaceable parameters** let you substitute variable data into batch files. Batch files utilize a special code (%n) that lets variable data be substituted in its place. You may need more than one variable parameter in batch files. A number (ranging from 1 to 9) follows the percent sign (%), giving you nine different variables (replaceable parameters) that may be substituted into your batch file.

The batch file above (CK.BAT) could include a single replaceable parameter (%1) that lets you specify a disk drive when you execute the batch file. Redo the COPY CON command, above, and change the CHKDSK command (in the batch file) to **CHKDSK %1**. Then, when the batch file is executed, the disk drive must be included as a parameter. The disk drive is substituted for the %1 entry in the batch file. For example, you could enter **CK B**: to display a CHKDSK status report for Drive B. The value B: is substituted for %1 in the batch file. Likewise, **CK A**: executes the CHKDSK command for Drive A.

Even though DOS doesn't have a "move" command, the batch file capability lets you create your own MOVE command. The following sample batch file (**MOVE.BAT**) lets you move a file from one location to another. It contains the following two commands that use two replaceable parameters:

```
COPY %1 %2
DEL %1
```

This batch file looks more complicated than the previous example because it contains two replaceable parameters. Each replaceable parameter in the batch file is replaced by the appropriate value when the batch file is executed. For example:

%1 represents the filename to be moved

%2 represents the location of the moved file

A batch file is executed when the batch file name with any required parameters is entered. Each parameter must be entered in the correct order, such as the values for %1, then %2, and so on. Suppose you wanted to use this new batch file to move BUDGET.TXT on Drive A to Drive B. To execute MOVE.BAT, enter:

```
A> MOVE BUDGET.TXT B:
```

The two parameters supplied during execution of the batch file (BUDGET and B:) substitute for the replaceable parameters (%1 and %2) in the batch file. In effect, the execution of this batch file is identical to entering the following two commands:

```
A> COPY BUDGET.TXT B:
A> DEL BUDGET.TXT
```

BATCH FILE COMMANDS

Besides the normal DOS commands available for use in batch files, several batch file commands give added power to batch file processing. Three such commands are:

- **REM** — Provides for remarks in batch files.
- **PAUSE** — Pauses to allow operator input into a batch file.
- **ECHO** — Sets the batch file echo feature on or off.

REM (Remark) Command (internal)

The **REM** (or remark) command lets you document your batch files, making them more readable. Remarks may display on the screen during execution of the batch file. To direct an inexperienced operator to insert a specific disk during the processing of a batch file, you could include the following command in a batch file:

```
REM INSERT THE DATA DISK INTO DRIVE B AND PRESS ENTER
```

However, the operator does not have time to read the message, much less take the appropriate action, before the next batch file command is executed. Fortunately, DOS provides a method for pausing execution long enough to allow the user to do something before continuing.

PAUSE Command (internal)

The **PAUSE** command is used to temporarily halt execution of a batch file. It halts execution at the PAUSE command in the batch file and displays the message **Press any key when ready . .** on the screen.

ECHO Command (internal)

Another batch file command used to improve communication during execution is the **ECHO** command. If you put ECHO OFF in your batch file, DOS will not display (echo) batch file commands during execution after that point. If you put ECHO ON in your batch file, all subsequent commands (including REMs) display on the screen. If you use the ECHO command with a message after it, the message is displayed, even if ECHO is off. The REM, PAUSE, and ECHO batch file commands are shown in Figure 9.2.

Figure 9.2

Sample Batch File (SS.BAT)

```
ECHO  OFF
REM    BATCH FILE NAMED SS.BAT
ECHO   PROCEDURE TO EXECUTE LOTUS 1-2-3
ECHO   PLACE THE LOTUS DATA DISK IN DRIVE A
PAUSE
CD\SS
LOTUS
```

The sample batch file in Figure 9.2 is executed by entering the batch file name (SS) without the extension. When DOS executes the first command in the batch file, it sets the echo mode off, so the REM command is not displayed. The REM command is displayed when the file is viewed with the TYPE command. Both ECHO messages display and the system pauses, waiting for any key to be pressed before continuing. Then the last batch file command is executed, the one that runs Lotus 1-2-3. Figure 9.3 shows you what the screen display will look like during the execution of SS.BAT.

Figure 9.3
Screen Messages from the Batch File (SS.BAT)

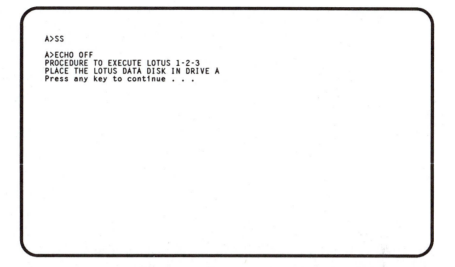

```
A>SS

A>ECHO OFF
PROCEDURE TO EXECUTE LOTUS 1-2-3
PLACE THE LOTUS DATA DISK IN DRIVE A
Press any key to continue . . .
```

Several additional points about batch files are worth mentioning:

- You can use **@ECHO OFF** to suppress the display of the ECHO OFF command. An @ at the beginning of any batch file line represses the display of that line.

- To issue a "beep" in a batch file (for alerting the operator to some action or problem), use **ECHO <Ctrl-G>**.

- You can enter the batch file command **ECHO:** to display a blank line on the screen.

- If you enter **ECHO OFF** at the system prompt, the system prompt disappears until you enter **ECHO ON**, or reboot the system.

- If you press **Ctrl-C** (Ctrl-Break) when a batch file is executing, DOS asks you if you want to terminate the batch job. Respond **Y** to halt the execution of the batch file and return to the system prompt.

- The COPY CON command is used to create small batch files, but it cannot be used for changing existing files. Use the EDIT command, discussed next, to create and change batch files.

USING THE EDIT COMMAND

Earlier versions of DOS relied on EDLIN, a cumbersome line-oriented text editor, to create batch files. DOS 5 has a full-screen, menu-based text editing facility called **EDIT**. This easy-to-use editor lets you create text files and change them as many times as you wish.

Creating a New File

The best way to learn about EDIT is to use it! Experiment with it by creating a new text file on Drive A called TESTEDIT.TXT. Enter the following command at the system prompt:

        A> EDIT A:TESTEDIT.TXT

If EDIT doesn't run, see if a file called QBASIC.EXE is in the same directory as EDIT.COM. If it is not there, make sure that it can be found in the current directory or in the search path. *QBASIC.EXE is required to run EDIT.* Once in EDIT, the screen should look like Figure 9.4. A Menu Bar is always displayed on the top line. It contains five pull-down menus for executing EDIT commands: File, Edit, Search, Options, and Help.

Figure 9.4
Initial EDIT Screen

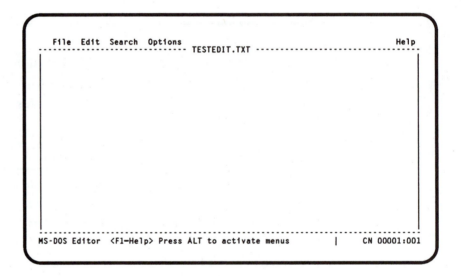

By pressing the Alt key and then the appropriate arrow keys, you can select a variety of tasks from the pull-down menus. Just as with the DOS shell, a pull-down menu is a small window that overlays a portion of your screen of text. It offers you a choice of menu options that are selected in several ways. One way is by pointing to a selection with the cursor and pressing the Enter key. You can also select an item by pressing the highlighted letter of the desired item, or by clicking on a selection with a mouse. Press the Esc key to exit from any menu. Figure 9.5 shows you what the pull-down menu for file operations might look like while editing an sample text file named PHONE.LST.

Figure 9.5
File Pull-down Menu in EDIT

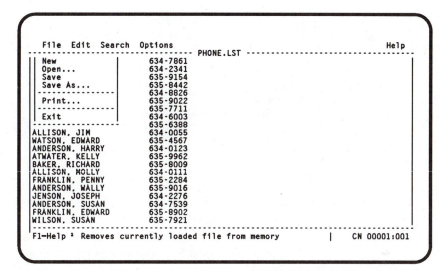

```
     File  Edit  Search  Options                                        Help
------------------------------------- PHONE.LST -------------------------------
   | New             634-7861
   | Open...         634-2341
   | Save            635-9154
   | Save As...      635-8442
   |-----------------|634-8826
   | Print...        635-9022
   |-----------------|635-7711
   | Exit            634-6003
   |-----------------|635-6388
ALLISON, JIM        634-0055
WATSON, EDWARD      635-4567
ANDERSON, HARRY     634-0123
ATWATER, KELLY      635-9962
BAKER, RICHARD      635-8009
ALLISON, MOLLY      634-0111
FRANKLIN, PENNY     635-2284
ANDERSON, WALLY     635-9016
JENSON, JOSEPH      634-2276
ANDERSON, SUSAN     634-7539
FRANKLIN, EDWARD    635-8902
WILSON, SUSAN       635-7921
-------------------------------------------------------------------------------
  F1=Help ª Removes currently loaded file from memory        |    CN 00001:001
```

Note that the bottom right portion of the screen in Figure 9.5 contains 0001:001. These numbers represent the current line number and current cursor position. They can assist you in entering and changing text. Enter the following three (3) lines of text so you can try some of the operations described in the following paragraphs. *Be sure to press the Enter key after each line.*

```
This text file is just for experimenting with EDIT.
It cannot be executed, but it can be displayed on
the screen using the TYPE command.
```

Text is entered in EDIT as in a word processing program with one major exception: each line is limited to 255 characters of text. Because EDIT is most often used with batch files, in which each line is usually quite short, this limitation is not a problem.

Using a variety of cursor movement keys, you can quickly jump around the screen to insert, change, or delete characters of text. Figure 9.6 identifies eight cursor movement keys.

When you initially edit a file, you are placed into the "insert" mode and the cursor shows as an underscore (_) character. If you want to overstrike existing text, press the INS key to switch to the "typeover" mode. In this mode, the cursor shows as a rectangular block. Use the Del key (or the Backspace key) to delete individual characters of text. Press Ctrl-Y to delete the line containing the cursor.

Figure 9.6
EDIT Cursor
Movement Keys

KEY	FUNCTION
Up arrow	Moves the cursor up one line on the screen.
Down arrow	Moves the cursor down one line on the screen.
Right arrow	Moves the cursor right one character.
Left arrow	Moves the cursor left one character.
Home key	Moves the cursor to the beginning of the line.
END key	Moves the cursor to the end of the line.
Ctrl-Home	Moves the cursor to the top line of the file.
Ctrl-End	Moves the cursor to the bottom line of the file.

If you need assistance, on-line help is available with the help feature. You can press the F1 key at any time to get context-sensitive information. This feature provides help for the operation you are attempting at the time you press F1. For example, if you were in the process of saving a text file and pressed F1, your screen would display information relating to saving files.

Using On-line Help

If you don't have access to any documentation on using EDIT, you can get continual on-line help in the top portion of the screen while working with text in the bottom portion. Whenever you press F1, the screen will be split into two windows, as shown in Figure 9.7.

Figure 9.7
EDIT Help Screen

```
┌─────────────────── HELP: Survival Guide ───────────────────┐
│ Using the MS-DOS Editor:                                 ↑  │
│   ·  To activate the MS-DOS Editor menu bar, press ALT.     │
│   ·  To activate menus and commands, press the highlighted letter. │
│   ·  To move between menus and commands, use the direction keys.   │
│   ·  To get help on a selected menu, command, or dialog box, press F1. │
│   ·  To exit Help, press Esc.                               │
│                                                             │
│ Browsing the MS-DOS Editor Help system:                     │
│   ·  To select one of the following topics, press the Tab key or the │
│      first letter of the topic. Then press the Enter key to see │
│      information on:                                        │
│   <Getting Started> Loading and using the MS-DOS Editor and the │
│                     MS-DOS Editor Help system               │
│   <Keyboard>        Editing and navigating text and MS-DOS Editor Help │
│ Tip:  These topics are also available from the Help menu.   ↓ │
├─────────────────────── PHONE. LST ──────────────────────────┤
│ SAMPSON, DAVID 634-7861                                     │
│ <F1=Help>  <F6=Window>  <Esc=Cancel>  <Ctrl+F1=Next>  <Alt+F1=Back> │
└─────────────────────────────────────────────────────────────┘
```

The larger window on top displays Help data, while the lower window (initially shown very small) is for entering text. To change the size of the windows, press the Alt key with the plus (or minus) key to increase (or decrease) the size of a window. A list of other commands is displayed on the bottom line of the EDIT screen. These commands are described below:

- **F1** — Displays context-sensitive help when you are editing text.
- **F6** — Moves from one window to the other.
- **Esc** — Exits from on-line help and displays text in a single window on the screen.
- **Ctrl-F1** — Browses forward through the Help information. If you have split windows, their size will vary based on the data displayed.
- **Alt-F1** — Browses backward through Help information.

Using the Pull-down Menus

Many of the EDIT commands, like commands to save an edited file or load a new file to be changed, use pull-down menus. Figure 9.8 describes these pull-down menu commands in EDIT. Menus and actions are chosen by typing the *boldfaced* letter shown, or by clicking on them with a mouse.

The Alternate key is used to select items from the Main Menu bar. When you are finished entering and changing text, press the **Alt** key and then the **F** key to display the pull-down menu for File. Because this is the first pull-down menu, you could have also pressed Alt and then the Enter key to do the same thing. Now press the **X** key to exit from EDIT. Enter a response of **N** when asked if you want to save the file. As you can see, using EDIT is an easy way to create and modify text files.

Using a Mouse with EDIT

You can use a mouse with EDIT the same way it is used with the DOS shell. Scroll bars are provided for browsing through on-line help information. Pull-down menus are accessed and actions selected and chosen by clicking on desired items.

Figure 9.8
EDIT Pull-down
Menu Commands

MENU	ACTION	DESCRIPTION
File	New	Completely erases everything in memory, letting you create a new text file.
	Open	Displays a dialog box that lets you select a file for editing. Use the Tab key to move to next area within a dialog box.
	Save	Backs up the current text and lets you continue editing.
	Save As	Copies the current text to disk using a filename you specify.
	Print	Sends the current text to the printer.
	EXit	If the current text is not saved, you are prompted to save it before exiting EDIT.
Edit	CuT	Extracts a block of text for later insertion. Hold down Shift key and use arrow keys to mark a block of text.
	Copy	Copies a block of text to another location.
	Paste	Inserts a block of text at the cursor location.
	ClEar	Deletes a block of text.
Search	Find	Locates a specified string of text.
	Repeat Find	Locates another instance of the previous character string used in the last Find action.
	Change	Replaces one string of characters with another.
Options	Display	Lets you change screen colors and display options.
	Help Path	Lets you specify the directory containing the EDIT.HLP file containing on-line Help information.
Help	Getting Started	Displays the initial entry screen to get the set of on-line Help information.
	Keyboard	Displays on-line help related to the keyboard.
	About	Displays the version of EDIT.COM.

**Chapter 9
Review
Questions**

1. What is the purpose of batch files?
2. How are batch files identified by DOS?
3. What are two different ways to create batch files?
4. When is an AUTOEXEC.BAT file executed?
5. What commands would you expect to find in an AUTOEXEC.BAT file?
6. How are variable data (parameters) included in batch files?
7. Why are REM statements used in batch files?
8. When are REM statements in batch files displayed?
9. What is the function of a PAUSE statement in a batch file?

10. What happens when you enter ECHO OFF at the system prompt?

11. What will be displayed on the screen when the following batch file commands are executed?

```
@ECHO OFF
REM SAMPLE BATCH FILE
ECHO PLACE WP DISK IN DRIVE A
PAUSE
:END
```

12. What does the term "full-screen text editor" mean?

13. What EDIT command moves the bottom line of a file in EDIT?

14. Define a pull-down menu.

15. How are the pull-down menus accessed in EDIT?

16. When using EDIT, what two keys let you delete a character of text?

17. If you are in the "typeover" mode, how do you insert characters of text in EDIT?

18. How can you access on-line help when using EDIT?

19. What File command erases the current text in memory?

20. What happens if you attempt to exit EDIT without having first saved the current text you are editing?

Chapter 9 Floppy Disk Lab Exercises

1. Use EDIT to create a text file.

   To begin this exercise, boot DOS, place your data disk in Drive B, and enter **EDIT B:LINEDIT.DOC.** You are now ready to create a new text file. The text to enter is shown in boldface below. Clarification comments are noted in parentheses.

   ONE (this is the first line of text)

   TWO

   THREE

   .

   . (continue with **FOUR** through **NINE**)

   .

   TEN

   (use the Up arrow key to move the cursor to the "F" in FOUR)

   (press the Del key five times to entirely delete that line of text)

   (use the Down arrow key to position the cursor at the beginning of the line of text after TEN)

   ELEVEN (this is the next line of text to be added)

TWELVE (this is the last line of text to be added)
(use the Up arrow key to move to the line of text containing THREE)
(press the End key to move to the end of that line)
(press the Enter key to insert a blank line of text)
FOUR (Enter key is not required here)
(press the Alt key to access the menu line)
(press the Down arrow key to view the pull-down menu)
(press S to save the file to disk with the filename previously given)
(press the Alt key and Down arrow key again to view the File menu)
(press X to exit the EDIT command)

2. Practice using EDIT by entering **EDIT B:LINEDIT.DOC** to recall previous text file.

   Delete the last two lines in the file, ELEVEN and TWELVE. Immediately after the line containing FIVE, insert a line containing ELEVEN. Then add two lines at the bottom of the file for TWELVE and THIRTEEN. Except for one line, the file of text should be in numeric sequence. See how long it takes to edit the file to make it all in sequence by numerical value. Save this file when you exit EDIT. What would happen if, after leaving EDIT, you sorted this file using the SORT command without the /R option?

3. Set up a batch file (**FORMAT.BAT**) to prevent anyone from formatting a disk on Drive A by mistake. This batch file will only permit FORMAT to format a disk on Drive B. Enter:

   RENAME FORMAT.COM FORMATB.COM   (renames the FORMAT command)
   COPY CON FORMAT.BAT (quickly creates a one-line batch file)

   FORMATB B:<F6>

   Note that the original FORMAT command was renamed so you could use FORMAT as the new batch file name. Then the batch file is used to execute the renamed format command (FORMATB) with the desired option, the formatting of Drive B only.

   Remove the disk in Drive B and enter **FORMAT** to execute the batch file just created. When you get the message to insert a blank disk in Drive B, press Ctrl-Break (or Ctrl-C) to terminate execution of this command. Figure 9.9 shows what the screen should look like after executing the batch file named FORMAT.BAT.

   Note: Before you continue to the next step, delete FORMAT.BAT and then rename FORMATB.COM to FORMAT.COM. Can you think of any other commands you would like to create?

Figure 9.9
Screen Display after Executing FORMAT.BAT

```
A>FORMAT

A>FORMATB B:
Insert new diskette for drive B:
and press ENTER when ready...^C


A>
```

4. Use **EDIT B:AUTOEXEC.BAT** to create a batch file on your data disk containing the following commands:

```
@ECHO OFF
REM SAMPLE INITIALIZATION PROCEDURE
DATE
TIME
ECHO ON
PAUSE  PLACE DATA DISK IN DRIVE B
DIR A: > B:DISKA.DIR
DIR B:
REM  END OF INITIALIZATION
ECHO OFF
ECHO  HAVE A NICE DAY
PROMPT  DATE IS $D $_TIME IS $T $_WHAT NEXT?
```

When you are done, execute this new batch file. Experiment with entering a few commands such as TIME, VER, and VOL with the new prompt. Then enter **PROMPT PG** to change the system prompt to display the current directory.

5. Use EDIT to build a simple batch file (**OFF.BAT**) that clears the screen when executed. Include the following three commands in this low-cost screen saver:

```
@ECHO OFF
CLS
PAUSE >NUL
```

The output of the PAUSE command, "Press any key to continue ..," is redirected to the NUL device so it will not display on the screen. After executing this command, press any key to return to the system prompt and continue working.

6. Create a short batch file (**TOP.BAT**) that will advance most Epson- or IBM-compatible printers to the top of the page. These printers recognize Ctrl-L as a form-feed character. If you are connected to an appropriate printer, you will be able to test this batch file. The batch file contains three commands as follows:

```
REM TOP.BAT TO ADVANCE PAGE TO THE TOP OF FORM
ECHO OFF
ECHO <Ctrl-L> >PRN
```

When typing the last line, press the spacebar after ECHO, then press Ctrl-L followed by another space before typing >PRN.

7. For additional work, build a batch file on your data disk with EDIT to create a new command for you. This batch file, called **MOVE.BAT**, lets you copy a file, give it another name, and then delete the original name. The new batch file should contain the following:

```
COPY %1 %2
DEL %1
```

This new batch file is executed by entering the batch file name (B:MOVE) followed by two parameters (for %1 and %2). The parameter %1 represents the original filename and %2 represents the new filename. Enter **B:MOVE B:TEST3.DIR B:TEST5.DIR**.

B:TEST3.DIR is now renamed B:TEST5.DIR. You could have specified that the new file was to be created on Drive A instead of Drive B.

This ends the Chapter 9 floppy disk lab exercises. Remove your disk(s) when you are done.

Chapter 9 Hard Disk Lab Exercises

1. Use EDIT to create a text file.

   To begin this exercise, boot DOS, place your data disk in Drive A, and enter **EDIT A:LINEDIT.DOC.** You are now ready to create a new text file. The text to enter is shown in Exercise 1 of the Floppy Disk Lab Exercises, above. Clarification comments are noted in parentheses.

2. Practice using EDIT by entering **EDIT A:LINEDIT.DOC** to recall previous text file.

   Delete the last two lines in the file, ELEVEN and TWELVE. Immediately after the line containing FIVE, insert a line containing ELEVEN. Then add two lines at the bottom of the file for TWELVE and THIRTEEN. Except for one line, the file of text should be in numeric sequence. See how long it takes to edit the file to make it all in sequence by numerical value. Save this file when you exit EDIT. What would happen if, after leaving EDIT, you sorted this file using the SORT command without the /R option?

3. Set up a batch file (**FORMAT.BAT**) to prevent anyone from formatting a disk on Drive C by mistake. This batch file will only permit FORMAT to format a disk on Drive A. Enter:

   RENAME FORMAT.COM FORMATA.COM   (to rename the FORMAT command)

   COPY CON FORMAT.BAT (to quickly create a one-line batch file)

   FORMATA A:<F6>

   Note that the original FORMAT command was renamed so you could use FORMAT as the new batch file name. Then the batch file is used to execute the renamed format command (FORMATA) with the desired option, the formatting of Drive A only.

   Remove the disk in Drive A and enter **FORMAT** to execute the batch file just created. When you get the message to insert a blank disk in Drive A, press Ctrl-Break (or Ctrl-C) to terminate execution of this command. Figure 9.9 shows what the screen should look like after you execute the batch file named FORMAT.BAT.

   Note: Before you continue to the next step, delete FORMAT.BAT and then rename FORMATA.COM to FORMAT.COM. Can you think of any other commands you would like to create?

4. Use **EDIT A:AUTOEXEC.BAT** to create a batch file on your data disk containing the following commands:

```
@ECHO OFF
REM SAMPLE INITIALIZATION PROCEDURE
DATE
TIME
ECHO ON
PAUSE PLACE DATA DISK IN DRIVE A
DIR C: > A:DISKC.DIR
DIR A:
REM END OF INITIALI  ZATION
ECHO OFF
ECHO HAVE A NICE DAY
PROMPT DATE IS $D $_TIME IS $T $_WHAT NEXT?
```

   When you are done, execute this new batch file. Experiment with entering a few commands such as TIME, VER, and VOL with the new prompt. Then enter **PROMPT PG** to change the system prompt to display the current directory.

5. Use EDIT to build a simple batch file (**OFF.BAT**) that clears the screen when executed. Include the following three commands in this low-cost screen saver:

```
@ECHO OFF
CLS
PAUSE >NUL
```

The output of the PAUSE command, "Press any key to continue ..", is redirected to the NUL device so it will not display on the screen. After executing this command, press any key to return to the system prompt and continue working.

6. Create a short batch file (**TOP.BAT**) that will advance most Epson- or IBM-compatible printers to the top of the page. These printers recognize Ctrl-L as a form-feed character. If you are connected to an appropriate printer, you will be able to test this batch file. The batch file contains three commands as follows:

```
REM TOP.BAT TO ADVANCE PAGE TO THE TOP OF FORM
ECHO OFF
ECHO <Ctrl-L> >PRN
```

When typing the last line, press the spacebar after ECHO, then press Ctrl-L followed by another space before typing >PRN.

7. For additional work, build a batch file on your data disk with EDIT to create a new command for you. This batch file, called **MOVE.BAT**, lets you copy a file, give it another name, and then delete the original name. The new batch file should contain the following:

```
COPY %1 %2
DEL %1
```

This new batch file will be executed by entering the batch file name (A:MOVE) followed by two parameters (for %1 and %2). The parameter %1 represents the original filename and %2 represents the new filename. Enter **A:MOVE A:TEST3.DIR A:TEST5.DIR.**

A:TEST3.DIR is now renamed A:TEST5.DIR. You could have specified that the new file was to be created on Drive C instead of Drive A.

This ends the Chapter 9 hard disk lab exercises. Remove your data disk when you are done.

CUSTOMIZING DOS

CONFIG.SYS File

ANSI.SYS File

RAMDRIVE.SYS File

CUSTOMIZING DOS

When DOS was introduced in 1981, the amount of RAM was severely limited compared with today's PCs. It was not uncommon to have a PC with only 256KB of RAM. DOS is designed to work with these smaller systems, but the default settings are not the most efficient for today's larger-RAM machines. Fortunately, DOS lets you reconfigure your system to take advantage of additional RAM.

DOS provides several different ways to customize your system. Even if your system has already been customized by someone else, you can use what you learn in this chapter to revise the customized settings. We will begin with the CONFIG.SYS file that automatically reconfigures your system according to your specifications during the boot process. Later you will learn how to use CONFIG.SYS to load instructions into additional memory, freeing up space in regular memory for processing applications.

CONFIG.SYS FILE

CONFIG.SYS is a special file of commands that lets you specify how your system should operate and be configured. Primarily, CONFIG.SYS allows you to control the way memory is used and to install device driver programs for controlling other devices.

During the boot process, DOS looks for a CONFIG.SYS file on the root directory of the disk used to boot DOS. If found, all valid commands in the CONFIG.SYS file are executed by DOS. If the CONFIG.SYS file is not found, the system is initialized according DOS default values. Booting with these default values should be avoided as they are too restricting. CONFIG.SYS is similar to a batch file in that it is a text file of commands, usually created with EDIT command. Here are the configuration commands that you will most likely use:

BREAK=ON tells DOS that you want it to also check for a Ctrl-C (or Ctrl-Break) entry from the keyboard during disk operations. By default, DOS only checks for a Ctrl-Break during keyboard or screen operations. Thus, if no screen or keyboard operations are being executed, pressing the Ctrl-Break key will be ignored by DOS unless BREAK is set ON.

BUFFERS=nn, where *nn* is the number of input/output buffers desired to improve disk performance. By specifying a relatively high number of buffers, you tell DOS to read a larger than usual chunk of data from your disk into RAM every time. Data stored in RAM is instantly available. The next time your program needs data, DOS checks to see if it is already in the RAM buffer. A recommended setting of 20 buffers will suit most circumstances. Each buffer uses 512 bytes (.5KB) of memory. It may require some experimenting to find the most effective buffer size for your system, especially if you are running sophisticated applications.

FILES=nn, where *nn* is the number of files that can be used at any one time by your programs. The DOS default is only eight. It is recommended that you have at least 20 files specified, as the number of open files include the hidden system files, COMMAND.COM, and Terminate-and-Stay-Resident (TSR) programs. Database applications often require 25 to 40 files open at a time.

SHELL=xxx, where *xxx* represents the command interpreter to be used. The default command interpreter is the COMMAND.COM file. Although the SHELL command can be used to specify a different command interpreter, SHELL is most often used to increase the size of your environment space. The DOS environment is space allocated to keep track of the values you assign to PATH, PROMPT, and DIRCMD variables. It also keeps track of other arbitrarily named variables used by application programs. As you install more programs that use the environment, such as Windows, you may run out of environment space. To increase the environment size from its default of 256 bytes to 512 bytes, add the SHELL command as shown in Figure 10.1. The maximum size is 32KB.

DEVICE=xxx, where *xxx* represents a particular device driver, such as ANSI.SYS, MOUSE.SYS, SETVER.EXE, or RAMDRIVE.SYS. Some device drivers are short programs that tell DOS how to handle input/output from a given device, such as a keyboard, disk, or mouse. A configuration command must be supplied for each device you wish to install. SETVER.EXE loads a table into RAM with the names of programs and the DOS version number with which each program is designed to execute. Chapter 11 explains how the SETVER command can modify this table to allow some older programs to run with DOS 5.

Figure 10.1 shows sample commands often included in a CONFIG.SYS file. Additional commands related to memory management are covered in Chapter 12.

Figure 10.1
Sample CONFIG.SYS File

```
REM  SAMPLE CONFIG.SYS FILE
BREAK=ON
FILES=25
BUFFERS=20
SHELL=COMMAND.COM /E:512 /P
DEVICE=C:\DOS\ANSI.SYS
DEVICE=C:\DOS\SETVER.EXE
DEVICE=C:\DOS\RAMDRIVE.SYS  360
```

ANSI.SYS FILE

ANSI.SYS is a device driver that acts as an interface between the monitor and DOS, as well as between the keyboard and DOS. It can be used to change the colors on the screen, the number of lines on the screen, or redefine the function keys on the keyboard. The American National Standards Institute (ANSI) has a special set of codes used to control the keyboard and monitor. These codes are activated by a special "escape sequence" of control codes. These codes can only be used when ANSI.SYS is installed. To install ANSI.SYS, include it as a device driver in the CONFIG.SYS file. If the ANSI.SYS file resides on your DOS subdirectory, use the full filename as shown in Figure 10.1.

Another common usage of ANSI.SYS is to change the way characters display on the screen, especially the colors. By using the PROMPT command to send DOS an appropriate escape sequence, you can change screen attributes by using the color codes listed in Figure 10.2.

Figure 10.2
ANSI Color and Attribute Codes

CODE	ATTRIBUTE SETTING	CODE	ATTRIBUTE SETTING
0	All attributes off	35	Foreground magenta
1	High intensity on	36	Foreground cyan
4	Underscored (monochrome only)	37	Foreground white
		40	Background black
5	Blinking on	41	Background red
7	Inverse (dark on light)	42	Background green
8	Invisible display	43	Background yellow
30	Foreground black	44	Background blue
31	Foreground red	45	Background magenta
32	Foreground green	46	Background cyan
33	Foreground yellow	47	Background white
34	Foreground blue		

The syntax of the PROMPT command used to change the attributes of the screen is complex. A dollar sign, the letter "e," and a left bracket ($e[) are used to send an escape sequence to ANSI.SYS. A semicolon (;) is used to separate the screen attributes and a lowercase "m" is used to terminate the attribute specifications. In addition, when you use the PROMPT command, you should include the desired system prompt, such as PG. Use the CLS command after a change of colors to clear the screen to the new colors.

Examples of Usage:

```
C:\DOS> PROMPT  $E[7m$P$G
```
(sets the monitor to display inverse characters; dark text on a light background)

```
C:\DOS> PROMPT  $E[0m$P$G
```
(resets the screen attributes back to normal)

```
C:\DOS> PROMPT  $E[37;44m$P$G
```
(displays white foreground characters on a blue background)

```
C:\DOS> PROMPT  $E[5m$P$G$E[0m
```
(causes the system prompt to blink and then returns to the normal mode for other text)

```
C:\DOS> PROMPT  $E[1mWhat Next?$E[0m
```
(turns high intensity on for the system prompt "What Next?" and then turns it off for other characters)

RAMDRIVE.SYS FILE

RAMDRIVE.SYS (VDISK.SYS in IBM DOS) is a RAM-resident device driver that lets you allocate a portion of main memory as a simulated disk. It is often called a RAM disk or "electronic disk." Access speeds in RAM are much faster than those of a hard disk, so files loaded into a RAM disk are accessed almost immediately. DOS always creates the RAM disk drive designator using the next available disk drive letter, normally as Drive D.

To install the RAM disk capability, you must have RAMDRIVE.SYS included as a device driver in your CONFIG.SYS file. You should specify more than the default of 64KB of RAM allocated to the RAM disk. If your RAMDRIVE.SYS file resides in your DOS subdirectory, include the CONFIG.SYS entry as shown in Figure 10.1 to establish a

360KB RAM disk. If you have additional RAM (2-8MB) you can create a much larger RAM disk. This subject is covered in Chapter 12.

As part of your AUTOEXEC.BAT file, you must copy any external DOS commands, batch files, and programs that you expect to execute most often into the RAM disk area. In addition, your PATH command should include the new RAM disk drive. For example:

```
COPY  C:\WP\WORD.*  D:
PATH = D:\;C:\DOS;C:\UTIL
```

Now you can execute your word processing program from Drive D rather than Drive C. It will execute much faster from the RAM disk than from your hard disk. Only program files should be loaded to a RAM disk, however. It is a dangerous practice to put data files on a RAM disk, because valuable data could be lost during power failures or surges. If you do have any data files on RAM disk, be sure to save them to perma- nent disk storage with the COPY or XCOPY command before turning off the CPU.

Chapter 10

Review Questions

1. Why would you want to customize the way DOS runs?

2. What do you think it means when someone says "DOS is downward (backward) compatible?"

3. What is the purpose of the CONFIG.SYS file?

4. How is a CONFIG.SYS file typically created?

5. What is the importance of increasing the default values for the number of buffers and the number of open files in DOS?

6. What file is the default command interpreter for DOS?

7. What is the DOS environment?

8. How do you increase the size of the DOS environment?

9. What is a device driver?

10. What is the purpose of the ANSI.SYS file?

11. Why is the PROMPT command often used to modify screen colors?

12. Specifically, what PROMPT command is required to display black text on a yellow background?

13. What must occur before you can execute a PROMPT command to change screen colors?

14. What device driver is used to create a RAM disk?

15. Why might it be dangerous to load data files to a RAM disk?

16. What command is used to load a mouse driver in DOS?

17. During what process are the commands in the CONFIG.SYS file executed by DOS?

18. Under what circumstances would you include BREAK=ON in your CONFIG.SYS file?

19. What color code (or codes) can be used to allow a password to be entered without being displayed on the screen?

20. Why do you think the CONFIG.SYS file is processed before loading the COMMAND.COM file during the boot process?

Chapter 10

Floppy Disk Lab Exercises

1. Assume you will be leaving your computer for a short time and want to discourage novice users from using your system. By entering ECHO OFF followed by CLS, your screen will become blank with just the flashing cursor. Experiment with this by running some commands without any prompt displayed. Then restore the prompt by turning ECHO back on.

2. Use EDIT to create a CONFIG.SYS file on Drive A that will provide for up to 25 files and 20 buffers in DOS, and install ANSI.SYS. If you have a color monitor, experiment with changing the colors of the screen. Don't forget to reboot to activate the ANSI.SYS file.

3. Create a batch file (**COLORS.BAT**) that will let you experiment with the screen colors once ANSI.SYS is installed as a device driver in the CONFIG.SYS file. This batch file is as follows:

```
REM  COLORS.BAT TO TEST SCREEN COLORS
PROMPT $E[%1;%2m$P$G
CLS
DIR /W
```

Install ANSI.SYS and execute COLORS.BAT several times, including the following three examples:

```
COLORS 33 40
COLORS 37 44
COLORS 30 46
```

This is the end of the Chapter 10 floppy disk lab exercises. Remove your disk(s) before you leave.

Chapter 10

Hard Disk Lab Exercises

1. Assume you will be leaving your computer for a short time and want to discourage novice users from using your system. By entering ECHO OFF followed by CLS, your screen will become blank with just the flashing cursor. Experiment with this by running some commands without any prompt displayed. Then restore the prompt by turning ECHO back on.

2. Use EDIT to create a CONFIG.SYS file on Drive A that will provide for up to 25 files and 20 buffers in DOS, and install ANSI.SYS.

3. Assume for the moment that you have a system with a hard disk and only one floppy disk. You want to make a backup copy of one of your floppy disks which contains data that is not on your hard disk. Create and test a batch file called C:\DOS\BKUP.BAT that will facilitate this process, one you anticipate performing often. The batch file should contain the following statements:

```
REM   BACKUP A FLOPPY DISK ONTO ANOTHER FLOPPY USING
REM   A ONE-FLOPPY, SINGLE-HARD-DISK SYSTEM.
REM
MD    C:\TEMP8765
REM   INSERT ORIGINAL FLOPPY IN DRIVE A:
PAUSE
COPY   A:*.*   C:\TEMP8765
REM   INSERT BLANK FLOPPY IN DRIVE A:
PAUSE
FORMAT   A:
```
(or FORMAT A:/F:720, if 720KB disk in 1.44MB Drive)
```
COPY   C:\TEMP8765\*.*   A:
REM
REM   RESPOND WITH "Y" TO THE ARE YOU SURE?   PROMPT
REM
DEL   C:\TEMP8765\*.*
RD    C:\TEMP8765
REM   END OF BACKUP
DIR   A:/P
```

4. Create a batch file (**COLORS.BAT**) that will let you experiment with the screen colors once ANSI.SYS is installed as a device driver in the CONFIG.SYS file. This batch file is as follows:

```
REM  COLORS.BAT TO TEST SCREEN COLORS
PROMPT $E[%1;%2m$P$G
CLS
DIR /W
```

Install ANSI.SYS and execute COLORS.BAT several times, including the following three examples:

```
COLORS 33 40
COLORS 37 44
COLORS 30 46
```

This is the end of the Chapter 10 hard disk lab exercises. Remove your data disk before you leave.

ADVANCED DOS COMMANDS

ADVANCED DOS COMMANDS

The more advanced DOS commands discussed here are not always needed. However, each command serves a purpose that may be required in certain circumstances. This chapter acquaints readers with several of these advanced commands so they can be used if the need arises. The following advanced DOS commands are covered:

FASTOPEN — Improves hard disk performance.

FDISK — Partitions a hard disk.

MODE — Modifies system parameters for input/output devices.

PRINT — Allows text to be printed while the computer performs other processing tasks.

SET — Sets the DOS environment variables.

SETVER — Identifies which version of DOS is to be reported for specific programs to be executed.

SYS — Makes a disk bootable with DOS.

ADVANCED COMMANDS

FASTOPEN Command (external, TSR)

Syntax: `[d:][path]FASTOPEN  d:[=size]  [d:[=size]]`

When DOS needs to locate files on a disk it must spend time accessing the disk's directory. The **FASTOPEN** command improves the performance of a hard disk by minimizing the number of disk accesses required. FASTOPEN uses RAM to store directory information from a specified disk. When FASTOPEN is activated, directory information is loaded into a RAM buffer by DOS, making it instantly available. This command is especially helpful if you have a large number of subdirectories and files.

FASTOPEN lets you specify more than one disk drive. A size parameter may be specified for each disk. The size controls the number of files and directories DOS can monitor in RAM. The default size is 48 entries, but a more practical range is 100–200 per disk. Each entry uses only 35 bytes, so a size of 150 would occupy about 22KB of RAM.

FASTOPEN is a terminate-and-stay-resident (TSR) program. This means that, once executed, it stays in RAM until you reboot DOS. It can only be executed once per session. If you issue FASTOPEN with several disk drives, the sum of all the sizes cannot exceed 999 entries.

Note: Defragmentation programs may not update disk file directory information that is temporarily stored in RAM by FASTOPEN. Thus, to avoid losing data when FASTOPEN is active, you should reboot immediately after running a program to defragment your hard disk.

Examples of Usage:

```
C:\DOS> FASTOPEN  C:
```
(increases performance of Drive C using the default size of 48 entries)

```
C:\DOS> fastopen  d:=100
```
(keeps track of up to 100 files and directories from Drive D)

```
C:\DOS> FASTOPEN  C:=100  D:=100
```
(increases performance of Drive C and Drive D using up to 100 entries from each)

FDISK Command (external)

Syntax: FDISK   (requires the DOS disk in Drive A)

The **FDISK** command creates and manages partitions on a hard disk. Even if you want just one partition, you must still run FDISK to configure your hard disk to use DOS. Normally, you will only have a single hard disk partition, devoted exclusively to DOS. However, a second partition could be used for another operating system, like UNIX. FDISK lets you create partitions, change from one partition to another, or delete partitions.

Each partition can be treated as a logical disk drive. Only one drive is active at a time. For example, you can partition your hard disk into two logical disks, Drive C and Drive D. Drive C would be the DOS boot disk containing all your programs. Drive D could be used to store all your data files. Having all data files on one drive simplifies the process of backup.

When you install a new hard disk, execute FDISK and chose Option 1, "Create Primary DOS partition." The system then asks you if you want to use the entire hard disk system for DOS. If you do, respond with a Y. Otherwise, respond with an N and consult the DOS Manual for further instructions. *Warning*: If you create a partition on an established hard disk, all existing data on the disk will be erased.

After the hard disk partition is established, you must run FORMAT with the /S option to make it bootable with DOS. Then you should copy COMMAND.COM and all the DOS external commands to a directory (i.e., \DOS) and store your DOS floppy disk for safekeeping. When this process is completed, you can boot the system from the hard disk.

MODE Command (external)

The **MODE** command sets the operational modes of the printer, monitor, keyboard, and communications ports. It allows you to reconfigure the way those system devices operate. Consequently, there are many different forms of the MODE Command. Three forms you might use are discussed below. Refer to a DOS manual for additional information.

Syntax for the Printer: `[d:]MODE LPTx cpl,lpi`

This form of the MODE command lets you specify how characters are printed for any printer that is IBM- or Epson-compatible. This way you can print 132 characters on a print line instead of the usual 80. The character x is the printer number (1–3), cpl is the characters per line (80 or 132), and lpi is the number of lines per vertical inch (6 or 8). When executed, MODE sends the appropriate control codes to the printer. The default settings are 80 characters per line and 6 lines per inch.

Examples of Usage:

`C:\DOS> MODE LPT1 132,8`
(sets the printer connected to LPT1 to print using compressed print at 8 lines per inch)

`C:\DOS> mode lpt1 132`
(sets the LPT1 printer to compressed print using the default of 6 lines per inch)

`C:\DOS> MODE LPT1 COM1`
(changes from parallel printer port LPT1 to a serial COM port)

Syntax for the Keyboard: `[d:]MODE CON RATE=x DELAY=y`

This form of the MODE command lets you change the speed of the keyboard on newer systems. This can speed things up dramatically, especially if you like to use your arrow keys to move around the screen or scroll the display screen. The rate at which the cursor moves can be from 1 to 32. The default rate is 20 on most keyboards. If you set the rate, you must also set the delay. The delay specifies the amount of time before the repeating key feature begins when you hold down a key. Valid values for the delay are from 1 to 4, representing 1/4, 1/2, 3/4, and 1 second, respectively. The default is 2 (1/2 second).

Examples of Usage:

```
C:\DOS> MODE  CON  RATE=1  DELAY=4
```
(sets the speed of the keyboard to be extremely slow)

```
C:\DOS> mode  con  rate=32  delay=1
```
(sets the speed of the keyboard to be extremely fast)

```
C:\DOS> mode  con  rate=20  delay=2
```
(returns the keyboard speeds to the original default speeds)

Syntax for the Monitor: `[d:]MODE  CON  [COLS=c]  [LINES=n]`

This form of MODE sets the number of lines displayed on a VGA screen or the number of columns displayed on any screen. The valid values for number of columns is 40 or 80. If you have trouble viewing characters on the screen, you can make characters twice as large with a setting of 40. The valid values for the number of lines are 25, 43, or 50. With this command you can have DOS display 43 or 50 lines rather than the usual 25. Length-sensitive DOS commands like CLS and MORE recognize the new screen sizes and adjust themselves accordingly. When using MODE to set the number of lines, the ANSI.SYS device driver must be installed via the CONFIG.SYS file.

Examples of Usage:

```
C:\DOS> mode  con cols=40
```
(sets the screen to display 40 characters per line)

```
C:\DOS> mode  con lines=43
```
(sets a VGA monitor to display 43 lines)

```
C:\DOS> MODE  CON  LINES=25
```
(resets the monitor to 25 lines)

PRINT Command (external, TSR)

Syntax: `[d:][path]PRINT  [/D:device] [/B:size] [/S:time]`

or

`[d:][path]PRINT [d:][path]filename[.ext]  [/P]  [/C]`

or

`[d:][path]PRINT  [/T]`

The printer operates extremely slow relative to the processing speed of computers. Thus, a small portion of computer resources (RAM space and clock time) can be allocated to printing (executing PRINT), while the majority of resources can be used for other processing at the same time. When you use the TYPE or COPY commands to print a disk file, you must wait until all printing is completed before executing another DOS command or application program.

You can avoid lengthy delays when you have long documents to be printed by using the **PRINT** command. Only files stored on disk in a printable format (ASCII text files) may be added to a print queue (list of files to be printed). Thus, PRINT cannot be used to print the output of a currently executing program. Most programs, however, have the ability to "print" to a disk file that can be later printed using PRINT.

PRINT is a terminate-and-stay-resident (TSR) program. Once PRINT is loaded, another program that you want to run at the same time can also loaded into RAM. DOS executes both programs concurrently, allocating a defined buffer size and amount of time to the PRINT program. The syntax for three commonly used forms of the PRINT command is given above.

The first form is used to initially load the PRINT program in RAM. This form lets you specify the device for printing, such as PRN or LPT1. If you do not specify a device name, DOS prompts you for one each time you execute the PRINT command. The first form also lets you define the buffer size (**/B**) and the amount of time (**/S**) allocated to printing. The maximum buffer size is 16,384 bytes (16KB) with a default of 512 bytes. Increasing the buffer size decreases the amount of RAM available for other programs, but may speed up printing. The maximum time slice is 255 slices per second, with a default of 2. Increasing the time slices can speed up printing but may slow down execution of other programs. If you want to use this form to change resource allocations, you must first restart DOS. This form is used only once per session.

The second form of PRINT is used as many times as required to add or delete files to be printed from the print queue. Wildcard characters are allowed. The **/P** option adds the specified file(s) to the queue. The **/C** option removes (cancels) the specified file(s) from the queue. The PRINT command prints files in the queue on a first-in, first-out basis. You cannot change or remove a file while it is being printed with PRINT, nor can you attempt to use the printer for another operation while PRINT is using the printer.

The last form of PRINT (**/T**) is used to remove (terminate) all print files in the queue.

Examples of Usage:

C:\DOS> PRINT /D:PRN /B:1024 /S:64
    (installs PRINT with a buffer size of 1KB and 64 time slices)

C:\DOS> PRINT C:\SS\WORK1.PRN
    C:\ACCT\BUDGET.TXT /P
    (adds two text files, WORK1.PRN and BUDGET.TXT, to the print queue)

C:\DOS> PRINT C:\SS\WORK2.PRN /P
    C:\ACCT\BUDGET.TXT /C
    (adds WORK2.PRN to the print queue and removes BUDGET.TXT from the queue)

C:\DOS> print /t
    (removes all files from the print queue)

SET Command (internal)

Syntax: SET [variable=[string]]

The **SET** command can be placed in the AUTOEXEC.BAT file to set any environment variables used by application programs each time you boot DOS. Many application programs utilize temporary work space on disk. Unless otherwise directed, these temporary files are stored in the current directory. When application programs experience problems during execution, the temporary work files may not be automatically deleted. Disk management can be facilitated if these work files are written to a specific directory, such as C:\TEMP.

To set an environment variable, use the SET command with an appropriate parameter, such as TEMP=C:\TEMP. To view the current environment, enter the SET command without any parameters. To clear a variable from the environment, enter the SET command with only the variable name and the equals sign.

Examples of Usage:

C:\DOS> SET TEMP=C:\TEMP
    (identifies the directory TEMP as the work space for any application program using TEMP as an environment variable)

C:\DOS> SET
    (displays the current environment settings)

C:\DOS> SET TEMP=
    (clears the TEMP variable from the environment)

SETVER (Set Version) Command (external)

Syntax: `[d:][path]SETVER`

   or

       `[d:][path]SETVER   filename   n.nn`

   or

       `[d:][path]SETVER   filename   /D`

The **SETVER** command allows you to add or remove program names from the DOS version table. This table is used by DOS to identify which version of DOS is to be reported for each program name in the table. Most programs will run correctly using DOS 5 even though they were designed to run with a previous version of DOS. But some will only execute if DOS 5 makes it think that it is running with a previous version.

Before you can use this command to modify the DOS version table, the table must be loaded into RAM during the boot process. *This is done using the DEVICE=SETVER.EXE command in the CONFIG.SYS file.* When you modify the table with SETVER, the changes are updated to a disk file, but the table in RAM is not changed. You must reboot after using SETVER to use the modified DOS version table.

The first form of SETVER (with no parameters) displays the DOS version table on the screen. You should pipe the output through the MORE filter (¦ MORE) to display one screen of output at a time.

The second form lets you add a filename with a desired version number to the DOS version table. Wildcard characters are not allowed. Suppose you want to execute a program (ACCT.EXE) that was designed to run with DOS 3.30 and will not run using DOS 5. In order to execute it with DOS 5, you must first modify the DOS version table as follows:

    `SETVER   ACCT.EXE   3.30`

Then, reboot to load the new DOS version table into RAM and run the program again. This technique will work for most older programs. The last form of SETVER is used to delete a file from the DOS version table. In both this form and the second form, only the filename can be specified; a disk drive and path are not allowed. To remove ACCT.EXE from the table enter:

    `SETVER   ACCT.EXE   /D`

Examples of Usage:

```
C:\DOS> SETVER | MORE
```
(displays the contents of the current DOS version table on the screen, one screen at a time)

```
C:\DOS> SETVER   CALC4.EXE   3.01
```
(adds CALC4.EXE to the table using DOS version 3.01)

```
C:\DOS> setver   calc4.exe /d
```
(removes CALC4.EXE from the DOS version table on disk but not in RAM)

SYS (System) Command (external)

Syntax: `[d:][path]SYS   d:`

SYS makes a copy of your DOS system files to another disk, such as a game disk. SYS transfers the two hidden system files and COMMAND.COM to the drive designated, making the disk bootable.

This command can be used to upgrade from one version of DOS to another. With SYS, you do not have to reformat your hard disk when you upgrade from one version of DOS to a higher one. Just boot the new version from a floppy disk and use SYS to transfer the new version's system files to the hard disk. Make sure that no old DOS commands remain on the hard disk, or you will occasionally get an "Incorrect Version" error message. When you upgrade to DOS 5 from a previous version of DOS, the INSTALL command automatically upgrades the DOS system files for you.

Examples of usage:

```
A> SYS   B:
```
(transfers your system files from Drive A to the disk in Drive B)

```
A> sys   c:
```
(transfers system files from Drive A to the hard disk, Drive C)

Chapter 11

Review Questions

1. What is the purpose of FASTOPEN?
2. What is a TSR program?
3. How does FASTOPEN improve disk performance?
4. What is the purpose of FDISK?
5. Why might you want more than one partition on your hard disk?

6. How do you make a partition bootable with DOS?

7. What is the purpose of the MODE command?

8. What does the command **MODE LPT1 8** do?

9. Specify the DOS command that increases the cursor speed to 50 percent faster than the default speed, keeping the delay for repeating characters at 1/2 second.

10. What command changes a VGA screen to display 50 lines?

11. What must occur before MODE can be used to change the number of lines on the screen?

12. What is the purpose of the PRINT command?

13. What is the effect of varying PRINT buffer size and time slices?

14. What type of files can be printed using the PRINT command?

15. What DOS command lets you view the environment?

16. Why might you want to create a variable in the environment called TEMP?

17. What is the purpose of the SETVER command?

18. What steps in DOS 5 are required to make a program called WRITIT.EXE think it is being executed with DOS 3.20?

19. What is the purpose of the SYS command?

20. What files are transferred to the designated disk with the SYS command?

Chapter 11

Floppy Disk Lab Exercises

1. Create a batch file (**B:PRT132.BAT**) that lets you print any text on the printer with compressed print (132 characters per line). This would be useful for printing wide documents on 8 1/2 x 11-inch paper. If your computer is attached to a printer, test the following batch file using a text file like AUTOEXEC.BAT as the replaceable parameter:

```
@ECHO OFF
REMPRT132.BAT TO PRINT COMPRESSED PRINT
REMPARAMETER USED IS THE TEXT FILE TO BE PRINTED
MODE   LPT1   132
COPY   %1   LPT1
MODE   LPT1   80
```

2. Create a batch file (**B:KB.BAT**) that lets you experiment with the cursor speed and repeating key delay. Use EDIT to create the following batch file with two replaceable parameters:

```
@ECHO OFF
REM KB.BAT TO TEST KEYBOARD SPEEDS
MODE CON RATE=%1 DELAY=%2
```

When the batch file is correct, test it using different values for the replaceable parameters.

3. Execute the SET command without any parameters to view the environment. Then change the screen to display 40 characters per line and execute the SET command again to see the results. Now change the screen to display 80 characters per line and 43 lines per screen. Run the SET command with these changes. Return the screen back to 25 lines per screen when you are done.

4. Use the first form of SETVER to display the contents of your current DOS version table, pausing at the end of each screen. You can do this only if the table is loaded into RAM. If your instructor agrees, modify the table to include TEST.EXE with DOS 3.30. Reboot and display the modified contents of the table. When you are finished, use SETVER to remove TEST.EXE from the table.

This is the end of the Chapter 11 floppy disk lab exercises. Remove your disk(s) before you leave.

Chapter 11

Hard Disk Lab Exercises

Follow the instructions for the Floppy Disk Lab Exercises 1–4, above, with one exception: the batch files you create will be on Drive A, rather than Drive B.

This is the end of the Chapter 11 hard disk lab exercises. Remove your data disk before you leave.

EXTENDED MEMORY MANAGEMENT

TYPES OF RAM MEMORY

MEMORY MANAGEMENT FOR 286 PCs

MEMORY MANAGEMENT FOR 386 AND 486 PCs

TASK SWAPPING WITH THE DOS SHELL

EXTENDED MEMORY MANAGEMENT

Most computers purchased today have at least 1 or 2 megabytes (MB) of main memory. Unfortunately, no matter how much memory your computer has, DOS programs only use the first 640KB. Any memory you have over the first 640KB is called **extended memory**. If your computer has 2MB of memory, it has 640KB of **conventional memory** and roughly 1.4MB of extended memory. DOS 5 includes an extended memory manager (HIMEM.SYS) that allows access to extended memory.

The primary objectives of this chapter are to explain:

- The different available memory areas
- How memory can be managed to significantly improve the performance of any system with extended memory
- Task swapping with extended memory

TYPES OF RAM MEMORY

The subject of memory management becomes increasingly complex as the amount of available memory increases. When PCs were limited to 640KB of memory, everything was crammed into one area, called conventional memory. With extended memory, there are several additional memory areas that can be used. Figure 12.1 identifies the areas of memory available on a 386 or 486 PC.

Figure 12.1
Memory Allocation for 386 and 486 PCs

0	640KB		1MB	1MB+64KB	4096MB
Conventional Memory Area		Extended Memory Area			
DOS 5 System Files	Application Programs and Working Data	Upper Memory Area		High Memory Area	XMS Area
		Video Buffers and ROM BIOS	TSR and Device Drivers	Rest of DOS 5 (64KB)	STORAGE FOR: ■ RAM disk ■ Disk cache ■ Print cache ■ XMS programs
(26KB)	(614KB)	(128KB)	(256KB)		

MEMORY MANAGEMENT FOR 286 PCs

The first 640KB of RAM on all DOS systems is called conventional (or low) memory. Low memory is used primarily for storing DOS and running application programs. Increasing the space available in low memory for application programs has two benefits: not only can you run larger programs, but smaller programs will execute more efficiently.

Depending on the type of microprocessor you have, it is possible to free up space in conventional memory. With a 286 PC, Terminate-and-Stay-Resident (TSR) programs and device drivers must be loaded in conventional memory; they cannot be loaded in the upper memory area as they can with 386 and 486 PCs (see Figure 12.1). However, if you have a 286 PC with at least 64KB of additional memory (beyond 640KB), a portion of DOS can be loaded into the high memory area (HMA). This is done by placing the following commands first in your CONFIG.SYS file:

```
DEVICE=C:\DOS\HIMEM.SYS
DOS=HIGH
BUFFERS=30
```

HIMEM.SYS is a device driver that manages all of extended memory, including the high memory area. By giving DOS the path to find HIMEM.SYS in the example above, you do not have to copy it to your root directory. The **DOS=HIGH** entry specifies that a portion of DOS (including buffers) is to be loaded into the HMA. Before you can use this command, HIMEM.SYS must be installed with the CONFIG.SYS file as shown above. The **BUFFERS** entry is shown here because it too is loaded in the HMA, rather than in conventional memory. Using the high memory like this will free up about 60KB of conventional memory.

MEMORY MANAGEMENT FOR 386 AND 486 PCs

The original design for microprocessor chips (limited to 1MB of addressing) reserved the lower 640KB for DOS and applications. The upper 384KB was reserved for video and ROMs. However, most systems use only part of the upper memory area. For about $70, you can purchase an easy-to-use memory management program like QEMM-386, to optimize memory on 386 and 486 PCs. Or, you can apply the information that follows for using DOS 5 to obtain an acceptable level of optimization.

System performance can be increased if you use DOS 5 on a 386 or 486 PC with at least 1MB of extended memory. For example, you can load DOS device drivers and TSR programs to the upper memory area. You can also create a RAM disk and a disk cache in extended memory, rather than in conventional memory. You must use a memory manager (included with DOS 5) that prevents different programs from using the same part of extended memory at the same time. Figure 12.2 shows a sample CONFIG.SYS file with memory management entries for 386 and 486 PCs.

Figure 12.2
**CONFIG.SYS File for
386 and 486 PCs**

```
DEVICE=C:\DOS\HIMEM.SYS
DEVICE=C:\DOS\EMM386.EXE   NOEMS
DOS=HIGH,UMB
DEVICEHIGH=C:\DOS\MOUSE.SYS
DEVICEHIGH=C:\DOS\SMARTDRV.SYS   1024
DEVICEHIGH=C:\DOS\RAMDRIVE.SYS   1024    /E
DEVICEHIGH=C:\DOS\ANSI.SYS
BUFFERS=10
FILES=30
```

EMM386.EXE is used to access the upper memory area on 386 and 486 PCs. *It is loaded with the DEVICE command,* rather than the DEVICEHIGH command. Windows 3.1, which has its own memory manager, and EMM386.EXE will coexist properly as long as you run Windows in real or 386 enhanced mode. If any of your application programs are designed to use **expanded memory (EMS)**, change the NOEMS parameter to RAM. Adding the parameter **UMB** to the DOS command tells DOS to manage the upper memory area. Before you can use the UMB parameter, however, EMM386.EXE must be installed as shown in Figure 12.2.

The **DEVICEHIGH** command is used to load ANSI.SYS, SETVER.EXE, and other device drivers into the upper memory area. It is also used to install the RAM disk (**RAMDRIVE.SYS**) in extended memory, using the /E option. In Figure 12.2, 1MB was allocated for the RAM disk. If you have IBM-DOS, use VDISK.SYS for the RAM disk driver.

Disk caching programs, like **SMARTDRV.SYS** (included with DOS 5) should also be installed in extended memory. When you use a disk caching program, reading and writing to disk goes through a RAM buffer area (a cache) first. The cache retains the data after it has been sent to its destination. Every time your system requests information from the hard disk, the caching program intercepts this information and copies it to the cache. If the same information is requested again, it is taken from the cache instead of from the disk. Because accessing from RAM is many times faster than accessing from disk, there is a substantial increase in performance. There is a potential problem, however. When you run program to compact (or defragment) your disk while a disk caching program is operating, you can lose data. To avoid losing data stored in the disk cache, always reboot your system immediately after defragmenting your hard disk.

EMM386.EXE must be installed before you can use extended memory for the disk cache. Because SMARTDRV.SYS has its own buffering capabilities, the recommended number of DOS buffers can be reduced to 10. Use the DEVICEHIGH command to load SMARTDRV.SYS in the upper memory area. The commands in Figure 12.2 create a disk cache using 1MB of extended memory. Figure 12.3 gives the recommended sizes for installing disk caches and RAM disks, based on the total amount of RAM.

Figure 12.3

Recommended Sizes for Disk Cache and RAM Disk

Total RAM	SMARTDRV.SYS (disk cache)	RAMDRIVE.SYS (RAM disk)
Less than 2MB	0	0
2MB	256KB	0
3MB	512KB	512KB
4MB or more	1024KB	1024KB

In addition to using the DEVICEHIGH command for device drivers, you can load a variety of useful TSR programs into the upper memory area with the **LOADHIGH** command. For example, there are TSR programs available that can automatically prevent computer viruses from being copied into your system from infected floppy disks. The sample AUTOEXEC.BAT file in Figure 12.4 includes the loading of three TSR programs: GRAPHICS, PRINT and DOSKEY.

Figure 12.4

Sample AUTOEXEC.BAT File

```
ECHO   OFF
PROMPT  $P$G
PATH D:\;C:\DOS;C:\WINDOWS;\C:\UTIL;\C:\MENU
LOADHIGH C:\DOS\GRAPHICS DESKJET C:\DOS\GRAPHICS.PRO
LOADHIGH C:\DOS\PRINT
LOADHIGH C:\DOS\DOSKEY
SET TEMP=D:\
MODE CON  RATE=25  DELAY=1
COPY \WP51\WP.EXE  D:
COPY \SS\123.*  D:
CD\MENU
AUTO
```

Whenever you add entries to your CONFIG.SYS and AUTOEXEC.BAT files, you must reboot DOS to activate your customized system. The GRAPHICS command above assumes you are using an HP Deskjet printer. The PRINT command lets you execute other programs while printing disk files. DOSKEY lets you retrieve previously entered commands from a buffer.

For a display of your computer's memory allocation, use the **MEM /C** command. Figure 12.5 shows you a sample listing of memory after DOS was booted using the CONFIG.SYS file in Figure 12.2 and the AUTOEXEC.BAT file in Figure 12.4.

Figure 12.5
Display of Memory Allocation with MEM /C

```
Conventional Memory :
   Name          Size in Decimal          Size in Hex
MSDOS              14160 ( 13.8K)              3750
HIMEM               1184 (  1.2K)               4A0
EMM386              8400 (  8.2K)              20D0
COMMAND             2624 (  2.6K)               A40
FREE                  64 (  0.1K)                40
FREE              628720 (614.0K)             997F0
Total   FREE :  628784 (614.0K)
Upper Memory:
   Name          Size in Decimal          Size in Hex
SYSTEM            163840 (160.0K)             28000
MOUSE              13968 ( 13.6K)              3690
SMARTDRV           14576 ( 14.2K)              38F0
RAMDRIVE            1184 (  1.2K)               4A0
ANSI                4192 (  4.1K)              1060
GRAPHICS            5856 (  5.7K)              16E0
PRINT               5776 (  5.6K)              1690
DOSKEY              4128 (  4.0K)              1020
FREE                 144 (  0.1K)                90
FREE               48304 ( 47.2K)              BCB0
Total FREE :      48448 ( 47.3K)

Total bytes available to
  programs (Conv+Upper):           677232      (661.4K)

Largest executable
  program size:                    628544      (613.8K)

Largest available upper
  memory block:                     48304      ( 47.2K)

3145728 bytes total contiguous extended memory
      0 bytes available contiguous extended memory
 797696 bytes available XMS memory
MS-DOS resident in High Memory Area
```

The first part of the listing identifies items loaded in conventional memory. The second part, labeled Upper Memory, shows what is loaded in the upper memory area. The last seven lines shown in Figure 12.5 provide an overview of the memory allocation.

Bytes available to programs (Conventional + Upper) identifies how much memory can be used by DOS applications in general. The next line defines the largest contiguous block of conventional memory available for a program. One of the major goals of memory management is to make this figure as high as possible. The next line gives the size of the largest contiguous block of upper memory available for loading additional device drivers and TSR programs.

Utilizing the extended memory area is another major goal of memory management. *Total contiguous extended memory* is the amount of memory beyond the 1MB boundary on a computer. The next line in Figure 12.5 (available contiguous extended memory) is a little confusing. This example indicates that all of extended memory is being managed by HIMEM.SYS. *Available XMS memory* is memory managed by HIMEM.SYS that is not yet used, but is available to programs that conform to the XMS (eXtended Memory Specification) standard. The last line of the MEM report informs us that a portion of DOS is loaded in the high memory area.

TASK SWAPPING WITH THE DOS SHELL

Another advantage of having lots of memory to work with is being able to load two or more application programs in memory and then switch between them; no quitting one program and loading another is required. This process, called **task swapping**, can be a tremendous timesaver. It is the next best thing to multitasking, in which multiple programs can be running at the same time.

From a practical standpoint, task swapping should only be used with extended memory. Thus, programs to be swapped should be loaded into extended memory first. In addition, task swapping with DOS 5 is only available through the DOSSHELL command. To activate task swapping, select the Options pull-down menu from the Menu Bar (Alt-O) and choose Enable Task Swapper (E). Once it is enabled, the Active Task List window appears in the lower right corner of the DOS shell screen, similar to what is shown in Figure 12.6. This is where the names of active programs will be displayed. A RAM disk (Drive D) is included as one of the disk drives in the upper left corner of Figure 12.6.

Figure 12.6

DOS Shell Screen with Active Task List

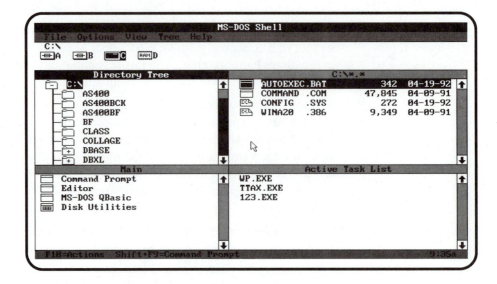

To add a program to the Active Task List:

1. Highlight a program file you wish to add.

2. Hold down the Shift key when you press the Enter key to select the program. This will add the program to the list, without actually starting it. The program will load when you switch to it.

3. Add as many programs to the Active Task List as you want.

To begin executing a program from the Active Task List:

1. Highlight the desired program name in the Active Task List.

2. Press the Enter key to execute the highlighted program.

3. If you have a mouse, you can double click on a name in the Active Task List to execute that task.

To switch to a different program in the Active Task List:

1. Press Alt-Tab and continue to hold down the Alt key while you release the Tab key. You will temporarily exit the current program and the name of the next program will appear at the top of the screen.

2. If this is the program you want to switch to, release Alt.

3. Otherwise, continue to hold Alt and press Tab to display the next program in the Active Task List.

4. When you switch back to a previous program, you will be dropped back into the program exactly where you left it.

To delete a program name from the Active Task List:

1. You can remove a highlighted program name from the Active Task List by pressing the DEL key.

2. A program name will be automatically be deleted from the list if you exit from the program normally (not with swapping).

To make task swapping faster and more efficient, create a RAM disk and copy onto it all the programs you want to place in the Active Task List. Because many application programs use temporary disk work space, you should include a SET command in your AUTOEXEC.BAT file as follows:

```
SET  TEMP=D:\
```
  (assuming the RAM disk is on Drive D)

This will enable DOS to keep track of temporary swap files in memory rather than on the hard disk. Another fine point regarding task swapping is worth mentioning. If you have an EGA monitor, you must include the following in the CONFIG.SYS file:

```
DEVICEHIGH=C:\DOS\EGA.SYS
```

This command is needed to enable DOS to save and restore an EGA screen when task swapping is used. It is not required for VGA monitors. Task swapping is not often required by many users, but those that need this capability find it very useful.

Chapter 12

Review Questions

1. Explain the difference between conventional and extended memory.

2. What kinds of files are often placed in extended memory?

3. Why is it beneficial to load DOS to the high memory area?

4. What command loads DOS to the high memory area?

5. What three commands must precede the DEVICEHIGH command in a CONFIG.SYS file to provide access to the upper memory area?

6. What DOS command is used to manage extended memory?

7. What DOS command loads device drivers into the upper memory area?

8. Why would it be beneficial to use a disk caching program?

9. How does a disk caching program work?

10. What is the disk caching program provided by DOS?

11. Why should you use the DEVICEHIGH command to install SMARTDRV.SYS?

12. What is the purpose of the LOADHIGH command?

13. What does the command **MEM/C ¦MORE** do?

14. Define the term "task swapping."

15. What DOS command entered at the system prompt is required to enable task swapping?

16. How are programs added to the Active Task List?

17. How do you swap from the current program to another in the Active Task List?

18. What two ways can be used to remove programs from the Active Task List?

19. What purpose does the command **SET TEMP=D:** serve?

20. With only 3MB of RAM, what are the recommended maximum memory sizes for a disk cache and a RAM disk?

Chapter 12

Floppy Disk Lab Exercises

1. To help you find out how your memory is allocated, create a batch file (**MEMORY.BAT**) on your data disk that redirects the output of the MEM/C command to a file viewed with the EDIT command. Add the following four commands to this batch file and execute it to test it for correctness:

```
@ECHO OFF
MEM/C  > MEM.TMP
EDIT   MEM.TMP
DEL    MEM.TMP
```

2. Use EDIT to create a CONFIG.SYS file on Drive A that will install SMARTDRV.SYS to use 128KB of conventional memory and will install ANSI.SYS. Then, reboot DOS. If you have a color monitor, change the screen to display red characters on a white background. If you have a VGA monitor, change the number of lines displayed to 43. Test these changes by displaying all the files on your DOS disk. Use MEMORY.BAT (from Exercise 1) to see where things are stored on your system now.

This is the end of the Chapter 12 floppy disk lab exercises. Remove your disk(s) before you leave.

Chapter 12

**Hard Disk
Lab
Exercises**

1. To help you find out how your memory is allocated, create a batch file (**MEMORY.BAT**) on your data disk that redirects the output of the MEM/C command to a file viewed with the EDIT command. Add the following four commands to this batch file and execute it to test it for correctness:

```
@ECHO OFF
MEM/C  > MEM.TMP
EDIT  MEM.TMP
DEL  MEM.TMP
```

2. Use EDIT to create a CONFIG.SYS file on Drive A that will install SMARTDRV.SYS to use 128KB of conventional memory and will install ANSI.SYS. Then, reboot DOS from Drive A. If you have a color monitor, change the screen to display red characters on a white background. If you have a VGA monitor, change the number of lines displayed to 43. Test these changes by displaying all the files on your DOS disk. Use MEMORY.BAT (from Exercise 1) to see where things are stored on your system now.

This is the end of the Chapter 12 hard disk lab exercises. Remove your data disk before you leave.

ADVANCED BATCH FILES

ADVANCED BATCH FILES

This chapter deals with applying advanced batch file commands to create sophisticated and powerful batch files. The following advanced commands are presented in this chapter:

IF — Creates branches within a batch file.

FOR — Repeats operations in a batch file.

CALL — Executes another batch file from within a batch file.

DEBUG — Allows the user to view and create executable files.

In addition, batch file techniques used to create effective batch files will be discussed.

BATCH FILE COMMANDS

IF Command

Syntax: `IF [not] condition  GOTO location`

Suppose you have an accounting system that is executed differently depending on the date (such as month-end, end of a quarter, and so on). **IF** is a batch file command that instructs the batch file to execute differently, depending on specified conditions. When the condition specified is true, DOS branches to the specified GOTO location. Otherwise, the next command in the batch file is executed. The NOT condition is interpreted in reverse, causing a branch only if the condition is false.

The IF command gives batch files the flexibility to branch depending on the various processing conditions that occur during execution. A GOTO command is used in the IF statement to direct it to branch to another location in the batch file. Branch locations must be named using the colon as the first character of the name, such as :OK or :END. Branch location names can be up to eight characters long (excluding the :) and can be placed anywhere in the batch file.

The most difficult part of using the IF statement is formulating the conditions that cause the desired branching. These conditions can be expressed in three different ways: EXIST file, ERRORLEVEL number, and String1==String2.

EXIST File Condition

If a data file required by a batch command does not exist, the **EXIST file** condition lets you modify the way the batch file executes. If the file exists (the EXIST file condition is true), the batch file can execute normally. Otherwise, appropriate measures may be taken to locate the correct file before proceeding. The following set of batch file commands verifies that a file exists before continuing:

```
:LOOP
IF   EXIST  A:FILEA.DOC  GOTO OK
ECHO  PUT CORRECT DISK IN DRIVE A
PAUSE
GOTO  LOOP
:OK
```
(The remaining batch file commands would go here)

If A:FILEA.DOC is not found by DOS, the batch file pauses and directs the user to place the correct disk in Drive A. Then the GOTO command branches back to the location named LOOP to test for the existence of the file. If found, the IF command branches around the error condition commands and begins executing the set of commands immediately following the location named :OK.

The use of a replaceable parameter for the specified filename gives additional flexibility. For example, the IF statement in the previous example could have been **IF EXIST A:%1 GOTO OK.**

Figure 13.1 shows a useful batch file that will execute a set of commands only if the date is a Friday. The rather complex set of commands creates a file (FRIDAY.TMP) only on Fridays, based on the system date.

Figure 13.1

Batch File to Execute Commands on Friday Only

```
@ECHO  OFF
REM VER is piped to DATE so DAT can be run without intervention.
VER ¦ DATE ¦ FIND  "Fri"  >DAY.TMP
REM  DAY.TMP can be created with no data filtered through FIND.
COPY  DAY.TMP  FRIDAY.TMP
REM  The COPY command will not copy a file with zero bytes.
IF  NOT EXIST  FRIDAY.TMP  GOTO END
DEL  FRIDAY.TMP
ECHO  IT IS FRIDAY!
(Place the Friday commands here)
:END
DEL  DAY.TMP
```

ERRORLEVEL Number Condition

The **ERRORLEVEL number** condition evaluates as true when the previously executed batch file command has an error condition equal to or greater than the number specified. Because ERRORLEVEL numbers vary by application, an ERRORLEVEL of 1 is normally used to signify an error. If an error has occurred, you can direct DOS to branch to the end of the batch file as follows:

```
IF  ERRORLEVEL  1  GOTO  END
```

This IF command directs DOS to branch to the :END location in the batch file whenever an error occurs. If ERRORLEVEL is zero (no errors), DOS executes the next batch file command in sequence.

String1==String2 Condition

When you execute a batch file with replaceable parameters, error checking is required to ensure the parameters were provided. DOS lets you check for missing parameters with the **String1==String2** condition. This condition is evaluated as true when the two specified strings are identical. The double equals sign is required. The technique for using this condition is best explained with an example. If the second replaceable parameter is missing in a batch file, you can direct DOS to branch to another location with the following statement:

```
IF  "%2" == ""  GOTO  ERROR
```

In this example, String1 is the value of the replaceable parameter (%2). Strings must be enclosed in quote marks. It is compared with String2, a null value (equal to nothing). When the batch file parameter is missing, the two strings are equal (nothing equals nothing), and the batch file branches to the location named ERROR.

FOR Command

Syntax: `FOR  %%v  IN(set)  DO  command [parameters]`

The variable (*v*) is a one-letter name preceded by two percent signs (%%). The *set* specifies one or more files (or text strings) that you want to process with the specified command. Parentheses are required around the set, and values in the set are separated by commas or spaces. The command is carried out on each successive value in the set by substituting the variable in the command with the set values. For example, the following batch file command deletes all BAK files in \WORD, \SS, and \HIST:

```
FOR  %%G  IN(\WORD,\SS,\HIST)  DO  DEL %%G\*.BAK
```

In this example, the three values in the set are substituted for the variable (*G*) in the DEL command. As a result, three commands are executed as follows:

```
DEL    \WORD\*.BAK
DEL    \SS\*.BAK
DEL    \HIST\*.BAK
```

The **FOR** command adds significant capability to your batch files. It lets you perform a single DOS command on a group (or set) of filenames. This is very beneficial, because some DOS commands (like FIND and TYPE) do not accept wildcard characters. Wildcard characters can be used in the set. Without the capability of the FOR command, those DOS commands must be entered multiple times to be executed with multiple files.

Suppose you wanted to copy all of your files from one disk to another in sequence by filename extension. Specifically, you wanted to copy all COM files, then all EXE files, and finally, BAT files. You could create the following batch file called **KOPY.BAT:**

```
@ECHO  OFF
FOR   %%F  IN (COM,EXE,BAT)  DO  COPY   *.%%F   B:
ECHO   COPY COMPLETE
```

You can obtain added flexibility by making the set of filename extensions replaceable parameters. In other words, you could substitute (%1, %2, %3) for (COM, EXE, BAT) in the FOR command. It is not mandatory that you use all of the replaceable parameters in a set. Using replaceable parameters the command **KOPY DOC TXT** would copy all of the DOC files from the current directory to Drive B, followed by all TXT files. This would be identical to entering the following:

```
COPY    *.DOC   B:
COPY    *.TXT   B:
```

Another use of FOR allows you to move down several levels of directories on your hard disk without having to find and enter the backslash key. Anyone who frequently uses different keyboards knows how frustrating it can be to locate the backslash key. To avoid this problem, enter the following command in a batch file called **TO.BAT:**

```
FOR   %%X  IN (\%1,%2,%3,%4)  DO  CD  %%X
```

Be sure to place this batch file in a directory that is specified in your current search path so DOS can find it from any directory. To change to \WORD\MEMOS\ HIST from any subdirectory on the hard disk, enter **TO WORD MEMOS HIST**. In effect, this would execute the CD command three times as follows:

```
CD \WORD
CD MEMOS
CD HIST
```

The FOR command can also be entered interactively at the DOS system prompt. When the FOR variable is used as a DOS internal command, only one % is used to identify the variable name. For example, to print the contents of all batch files on Drive B, you could execute the following FOR command at the system prompt:

```
A> for %x in (b:*.bat) do type %x >prn
```

CALL Command

Syntax: `CALL [d:][path] filename [parameters]`

Because a batch file is an executable "command," batch files can be executed from within another batch file. However, when you include just the batch file name for execution, DOS transfers control to that batch file with no way to return to the original batch file. This is all right if the batch file to which you want to transfer is the last command in the original batch file, but it becomes a problem if there are other commands to execute in the original batch file. The **CALL** command resolves this problem by returning to the next command in the first batch file after executing the second batch file.

You can use CALL to specify another batch file to be executed anywhere in the original batch file. You can also include any parameters required by that batch file. When the "called" batch file is finished, DOS continues processing the remaining commands in the original batch file. In the following example, when the batch file DOACCT.BAT is finished, the remaining commands in the original batch file will be executed.

```
PAUSE  PLACE ACCOUNTING DATA DISK IN DRIVE A
CALL  DOACCT
```
(command to be executed after DOACCT.BAT)

CREATING EFFECTIVE BATCH FILES

What is an effective batch file? Any batch file that improves your ability to be productive and minimizes errors is a likely candidate. Here we cover several ways to create effective batch files.

One technique is to create batch files that give you added protection from making a mistake. For example, when you want to delete a group of files using wildcard characters, you should always display a list of the files you want to delete before they are actually deleted. The batch file (PURGE.BAT) in Figure 13.2 does this and can be used as an effective substitute for the DEL command.

Figure 13.2

Batch File to Display Files Being Deleted

```
@ECHO OFF
REM   IMPROVED DEL COMMAND (PURGE.BAT)
DIR   %1/W
ECHO THESE FILES WILL BE DELETED (PRESS CTRL-BRK TO ABORT)
PAUSE
DEL   %1
```

Another technique is to create a batch file that will automatically respond to DOS prompts. For example, when you format a disk, change the volume label, or delete all files on a directory, DOS requests information to continue. If you want to automatically enter a single response, you can use ECHO to pipe a response to a DOS command. The following command automatically deletes all files on the default directory without waiting for a response to the "Are you sure?" message:

```
ECHO Y ¦ DEL *.* >NUL
```

The screen output "Are you sure (Y/N)?" is redirected to NUL so it will not be displayed on the screen during the delete operation. If you have multiple responses to a DOS command in a batch file, you must use a different technique.

To automatically enter multiple responses in a batch file, you can create a text file containing the responses and redirect it to a DOS command. Suppose you wanted to FORMAT a single data disk with the volume label DATADISK. Using EDIT, you would create a file called RESP.DAT as follows:

```
<Enter>
DATADISK<Enter>
N<Enter>
```

This text file contains the responses necessary to automatically execute the FORMAT command. The first response (just an Enter key) tells DOS that the disk is in the drive and ready to be formatted. The next response supplies the volume label. The last response tells DOS that there are no more disks to be formatted. Redirection is used to input responses to the FORMAT command when needed. The following batch file commands can then be used to format a data disk automatically:

```
ECHO   PLACE DISK TO BE FORMATTED IN DRIVE %1
PAUSE
FORMAT   %1   <RESP.DAT
```

It is also very important that batch files detect errors, especially when replacement parameters are used. Suppose you want a batch file that restricts the user to formatting only Drive A. In other words, you want to control the way FORMAT is executed. First you must rename FORMAT.COM to something else, like FORM.COM. Then you can create a batch file (**FORMAT.BAT**) that executes whenever FORMAT is entered as a command. Figure 13.3 shows the commands in FORMAT.BAT. Whenever you enter FORMAT and the first parameter is missing, or is other than A: or a:, it is rejected by this batch file.

Figure 13.3

Batch File to Format Drive A Only

```
@ECHO OFF
REM   FORMAT.BAT TO FORMAT ONLY DRIVE A
IF    "%1" == "" GOTO ERROR
IF   %1==A:   GOTO OK
IF   %1==a:   GOTO OK
ECHO   YOU ARE NOT ALLOWED TO FORMAT DRIVE %1
GOTO   END
:OK
REM   A SECOND REPLACEABLE PARAMETER LETS
REM   YOU INCLUDE OPTIONS LIKE   /F:720
FORM   %1   %2
GOTO   END
:ERROR
ECHO   YOU MUST ENTER THE DRIVE TO FORMAT
:END
```

To prevent new programs you install on your computer from changing your AUTOEXEC.BAT file without your knowledge, place your automatic execution commands in another batch file, like ALIAS.BAT. Then include only two lines in your AUTOEXEC.BAT file as follows:

```
@ECHO OFF
ALIAS.BAT
```

Sometimes you may need to execute a batch file differently depending on a user response. In order to do this type of selective branching, you must have the ability to capture a keystroke from the user. DOS has a powerful command called DEBUG that can be used for a variety of tasks, including creating executable programs.

DEBUG COMMAND

DEBUG is a machine-level utility program for snooping around in DOS and making all sorts of subtle modifications. In addition to creating executable programs, it can display memory values, modify them, and view executable files like those with EXE or COM extensions. If you know what you are doing, you can use DEBUG to recover lost disk files and edit the COMMAND.COM file. In fact, a whole chapter could be devoted to this extraordinary command. Our intent, however, is to introduce you to DEBUG, not to make you a DEBUG expert!

One use of DEBUG is to view the contents of an executable file. To view the contents of the FORMAT command, enter **DEBUG FORMAT.COM**. The first thing you would see displayed on the screen is the hyphen (-), which is the DEBUG command prompt. Enter the DEBUG command **D** to display 128 bytes of the file. Figure 13.4 shows you what a portion of the screen looks like after pressing D 15 or 16 times.

Figure 13.4
Screen Display of DEBUG

```
269B:07A0  00 FF 00 00 00 58 00 01-00 B0 00 01 00 FF 00 00   .....X..........
269B:07B0  00 59 00 01 00 BB 00 02-00 FF A6 04 B2 00 0F 00   .Y..............
269B:07C0  B0 FF FF FF FF 04 00 B2-00 08 00 B0 FF FF FF FF   ................
269B:07D0  04 00 B2 00 08 00 B0 FF-08 00 B0 00 0C 00 B0 FF   ................
269B:07E0  FF FF FF 00 00 00 00 00-00 00 0D 0A 00 00 00 00   ................
269B:07F0  00 0A 00 14 00 B2 24 41-00 B0 4D 53 20 44 4F 53   ......$A..MS DOS
-D
269B:0800  20 56 65 72 73 69 6F 6E-20 35 2E 30 30 20 28 43    Version 5.00 (C
269B:0810  29 43 6F 70 79 72 69 67-68 74 20 31 39 38 31 2D   )Copyright 1981-
269B:0820  31 39 39 31 20 4D 69 63-72 6F 73 6F 66 74 20 43   1991 Microsoft C
269B:0830  6F 72 70 20 4C 69 63 65-6E 73 65 64 20 4D 61 74   orp Licensed Mat
269B:0840  65 72 69 61 6C 20 2D 20-50 72 6F 70 65 72 74 79   erial - Property
269B:0850  20 6F 66 20 4D 69 63 72-6F 73 6F 66 74 20 41 6C    of Microsoft Al
269B:0860  6C 20 72 69 67 68 74 73-20 72 65 73 65 72 76 65   l rights reserve
269B:0870  64 20 00 00 00 00 00 7D-00 B2 20 0D 00 B0 46 4D   d .....}.. ...FM
-D
269B:0880  54 2E 45 58 45 00 80 09-00 B2 00 04 01 B0 D0 06   T.EXE...........
269B:0890  00 01 01 F4 06 0F FD 06-09 07 15 07 21 07 2D 07   ............!.-.
269B:08A0  39 07 45 07 51 07 5D 07-6E 07 7F 07 92 07 9E 07   9.E.Q.].n.......
269B:08B0  AA 07 B6 07 00 00 01 00-00 00 09 4B 08 00 81 20   ...........K...
269B:08C0  01 00 1D 09 4B 08 01 2F-56 00 00 00 00 00 0D 09   ....K../V.......
269B:08D0  4B 08 01 2F 53 00 00 00-00 00 0D 09 4B 08 01 2F   K../S.......K../
269B:08E0  34 00 00 00 00 00 0D 09-4B 08 01 2F 31 00 00 00   4.......K../1...
269B:08F0  00 00 0D 09 4B 08 01 2F-38 00 00 00 00 00 0D 09   ....K../8.......
-
```

The DEBUG display is in two parts. The left side displays the data in hexadecimal (base 16) form and the right side shows the character translations in ASCII. You can keep on pressing D as long as you want to continue displaying the file. Use the DEBUG command **Q** (Quit) to exit DEBUG.

Because DEBUG is designed for advanced DOS users, novice users typically find it overly technical and complicated. But don't get discouraged. You can find detailed instructions on how to use DEBUG in the DOS manual or other reference works. In this chapter, Figure 13.5 contains the DEBUG instructions for creating an executable program to capture a keystroke from a user. The explanatory text in parenthesis must *not* be keyed.

Figure 13.5
DEBUG Commands to Create GETKEY.COM

```
DEBUG (execute the DEBUG command)
-E 100 B4 00 CD 16 B4 4C CD 21 (Enter
instructions)
-N GETKEY.COM (Name the executable program GETKEY.COM)
-RCX (change the size Register, CX)
:8 (set the size to 8 bytes)
-W (Write the new file to disk)
-Q (Quit DEBUG)
```

After GETKEY.COM is created you can use it in a batch file to identify a keystroke from a user. Strange as it may seem, ERRORLEVEL codes are used to identify a keystroke entered in response to the GETKEY program. Some of the ERRORLEVEL codes you may wish to use are shown in Figure 13.6.

Figure 13.6
Sample ERRORLEVEL Codes

```
      0  =  NUL
      7  =  Bell (Ctrl-G)
     13  =  Enter key
     27  =  Esc key
     32  =  Spacebar
  48-57  =  Digits (0-9)
     63  =  Question mark (?)
  65-90  =  Uppercase alphabet (A-Z)
 97-122  =  Lowercase alphabet (a-z)
```

When testing for a specific ERRORLEVEL code with the IF command, DOS looks for a code equal to or greater than the code specified to evaluate the condition as true. For example, to identify the Enter key (ERRORLEVEL 13), you must test for a code that is 13 or more, but not 14 or more. Figure 13.7 shows you a batch file you can create and test to see how ERRORLEVEL testing works.

Figure 13.7
Example of ERRORLEVEL Testing

```
@ECHO OFF
:TOP
ECHO   BREAK OUT OF THIS LOOP BY PRESSING THE ENTER KEY ONLY
GETKEY
IF  ERRORLEVEL 13  IF NOT  ERRORLEVEL 14  GOTO CONT
GOTO TOP
:CONT
```

Although batch file processing adds power and convenience to the operation of a computer, it is not meant to be used as a replacement for a true programming language, such as C or BASIC. DOS batch files are relatively inefficient because each command must be interpreted by DOS during execution. However, for the user who does not want to spend the time to learn a programming language, batch files offer an easy way to improve the overall efficiency of the computer system.

Chapter 13

Review Questions

1. What is the main purpose of the IF statement in a batch file?
2. What does a GOTO statement do in a batch file?
3. How do you identify a location to branch to in a batch file?
4. What does the EXIST File condition let you do in a batch file?
5. What does an ERRORLEVEL code of zero mean?
6. How can a batch file detect a missing replaceable parameter?
7. Explain how the FOR command works.
8. What FOR command deletes all BAK and TMP files in the current directory?
9. When can wildcard characters be used in the FOR command?
10. What does the command **FOR %X in (*.BAT) DO FIND "PATH" %X** do?

11. What is the purpose of the CALL command?

12. How can you automatically enter a single predefined response to a DOS command in a batch file?

13. How can you automatically enter multiple predefined responses to a DOS command in a batch file?

14. Under what conditions would DOS be able to execute a batch file named CHKDSK.BAT?

15. What happens when you redirect screen output to NUL?

16. Specify the IF command used after GETKEY.COM to branch to a location named END when the number 1 is entered from the keyboard.

17. What are three things you can do with the DEBUG command?

18. List at least four DEBUG commands.

19. How is the FOR command executed in a batch file differently than from the system prompt?

20. List the batch file commands that will delete all the BAK files from up to five given directories on Drive C.

Chapter 13

Floppy Disk Lab Exercises

1. Rather than purchasing a utility program to search your hard disk for a particular filename, you can create your own customized batch file named PHIND.BAT. You cannot call this file FIND.BAT because entering the batch file name of FIND would cause DOS to execute FIND.COM. Create the following batch file (without the explanatory comments):

   @ECHO OFF (turn echo off)

   IF "%1"=="" GOTO ERROR (if no parameter, branch to ERROR)

   CHKDSK B:/V | FIND "%1"(send all filenames on Drive B to filter)

   GOTO END (branch around the error message to END)

   :ERROR (branch location labeled ERROR)

   ECHO PARAMETER REQUIRED (display error message)

   :END (branch location labeled END)

   This useful batch file directs CHKDSK to locate every filename on Drive B and pipe it to FIND. FIND filters out all filenames not containing the characters specified by the variable parameter (%1).

The IF test lets the batch file skip over the CHKDSK and FIND operations if no parameter is included with PHIND. Figure 13.8 shows you what the screen might look like if you executed PHIND.BAT, first with no parameter, and then with TEST as a parameter.

Figure 13.8

Screen Display after Executing PHIND.BAT

```
A>PHIND
PARAMETER REQUIRED
A>PHIND TEST
B:\TEST.1
B:\TEST.3
B:\TEST.4
B:\TEST.ROF
B:\DOS\TEST.1
B:\DOS\TEST.3
B:\DOS\TEST.4
B:\DOS\TEST.ROF
B:\TEST1.DIR
B:\TEST2.DIR
B:\TEST3.DIR
A>
```

2. Create the following batch file called SUPERMAT.BAT that will format a disk with the /S option and automatically copy FORMAT.COM and CHKDSK.COM to the newly formatted disk. This would be a useful program for formatting floppy disks that are to be bootable and contain the FORMAT and CHKDSK commands. Specific application programs could also be copied to these bootable disks. If you have a blank disk, execute this program to see how it works.

```
@ECHO  OFF
REM  SUPERMAT.BAT USED TO CREATE BOOTABLE DISKS
CLS
FORMAT  B:/S
COPY  FORMAT.COM  B: >NUL
COPY  CHKDSK.COM  B: >NUL
DIR  B:
ECHO  END OF SUPERMAT
```

3. Create an executable program (with DEBUG) that toggles off the Num Lock key on your keyboard. Then you could include it in your AUTOEXEC.BAT file to automatically turn off the Num Lock key

every time you booted your computer. This program (NONUM.COM) can be easily created in two rather unusual steps as follows:

- The first step uses EDIT to create a text file of DEBUG commands needed to create NONUM.COM. Create this text file (NONUM.DAT) exactly as shown in Figure 13.9, including the blank line.

- The next step is to execute DEBUG and redirect the DEBUG commands contained in NONUM.DAT to create NONUM.COM. Enter the command **DEBUG <NONUM.DAT** at the system prompt.

Figure 13.9
NONUM.DAT

```
a 100
mov ax,0000
mov ds,ax
and byte ptr[0417],df
int 20
   (blank line here)
rcx
c
n nonum.com
w
q
```

After you create NONUM.COM, test it on your computer with different settings of the Num Lock key. Whenever you enter NONUM, the Num Lock key is toggled off. Depending on your keyboard, the Num Lock status light may not be affected by this command.

4. Use the following DEBUG commands to create an executable program that can be used to send a form feed (FF) control character to an IBM- or Epson-compatible printer:

```
-N  FF.COM
-E  0100  B4  05  B2  0C  CD  21  CD  20
-RCX
:8
-W
-Q
```

If you are connected on-line to an IBM- or Epson-compatible printer, test your new command by entering **FF** at the system prompt. If everything is correct, your printer should advance to the top of page.

5. Sometimes users want protection against other users, particularly novice users, accessing their system without permission. Although

few protection systems can deter an experienced user, the batch file in Figure 13.10 will help. When these commands are placed in the beginning of your AUTOEXEC.BAT file, most novice users will not be able to get past the boot process without the secret password.

Figure 13.10
Password Protection
Batch File

```
@ECHO   OFF
REM   PASSWORD PROTECTION
PROMPT   Fatal Disk Error #23 -- Reboot
:TOP
CLS
ECHO   Unrecoverable read error on Drive A:
ECHO   Abort, Retry, or Fail?
GETKEY
IF  ERRORLEVEL 63   IF NOT ERRORLEVEL 64   GOTO END
:CAUSE THE DISK TO SPIN FOR A WHILE
COPY   COMMAND.COM   COMMAND.BAK >NUL
DEL   COMMAND.BAK
GOTO   TOP
:END
(Place rest of  AUTOEXEC.BAT file commands here)
```

Have you determined the purpose of the PROMPT command in this batch file yet? If you terminate execution of the batch file with Ctrl-Break, the reason may become evident to you.

This concludes the Chapter 13 floppy disk lab exercises. When you are finished, remove your disk(s). We hope you enjoyed learning DOS and doing the exercises in this text. Best wishes for better computing!

Chapter 13

Hard Disk Lab Exercises

Follow the instructions for the floppy disk lab exercises above, making the following changes where applicable:

• Change Drive B (data disk) to Drive A in the first two batch files (PHIND.BAT and SUPERMAT.BAT).

• Change Drive A (DOS disk) to Drive C in the last exercise.

This concludes the Chapter 13 hard disk lab exercises. When you are finished, remove your data disk. We hope you enjoyed learning DOS and doing the exercises in this text. Best wishes for better computing!

SUMMARY OF DOS COMMANDS

This list includes commands covered in the text and others that you might need to use.

COMMAND	VER.	CHAPTER	BRIEF DESCRIPTION OF COMMAND
APPEND	3.2	—	Sets a search path for data files (TSR).
ASSIGN	2.0	—	Assigns a disk drive letter to another drive.
ATTRIB	3.0	6	Sets/displays attributes of a file.
BACKUP	2.0	7	Backs up files from disk.
CD	2.0	7	Changes directories (CHDIR).
CHKDSK	1.0	6	Checks for file fragmentation on a disk.
CLS	2.0	5	Clears the screen.
COMMAND	1.0	—	Supplies internal DOS commands.
COMP	1.0	—	Compares two files for differences.
COPY	1.0	5	Copies specified files.
DATE	1.1	5	Displays and sets the system date.
DEBUG	2.0	13	Machine-level utility program for DOS.
DEL	1.0	5	Deletes (erases) specified files.
DIR	1.0	5	Displays directory entries.
DISKCOMP	1.0	—	Compares two disks.
DISKCOPY	1.0	6	Makes an exact copy of a disk.
DOSKEY	5.0	8	Recalls and edits previous commands.
DOSSHELL	4.0	4	Starts the graphical interface to DOS.
EDIT	5.0	9	Executes the DOS full-screen editor.

ERASE	1.0	5	Identical to DELETE command.
EXIT	2.0	4	Exits DOS and returns to an application program.
FASTOPEN	3.3	11	Improves hard disk performance (TSR).
FDISK	2.0	11	Partitions a hard disk for DOS.
FIND	2.0	8	Searches for a given string of text.
FORMAT	1.0	3	Formats a disk to receive DOS files.
GRAPHICS	2.0	12	Prepares DOS for printing graphics (TSR).
HELP	5.0	3	Provides on-line help for DOS 5.
JOIN	3.0	—	Treats a disk drive as a subdirectory.
LABEL	3.0	6	Labels a disk.
LOADHIGH	5.0	12	Loads TSR programs into high memory.
MD	2.0	7	Makes a directory (MKDIR).
MEM	4.0	12	Displays amount of used and free memory.
MIRROR	5.0	—	Records data for UNDELETE and UNFORMAT.
MODE	1.0	11	Modifies system parameters.
MORE	2.0	8	Displays output one screen at a time.
PATH	2.0	7	Sets a command search path.
PRINT	2.0	11	Prints a file concurrently.
PROMPT	2.0	7	Assigns the system prompt.
RD	2.0	7	Removes a directory (RMDIR).
RECOVER	2.0	6	Recovers a bad disk or file.
REN	1.0	5	Renames a file (RENAME).
REPLACE	3.2	—	Facilitates updating of files.

RESTORE	2.0	7	Restores previously backed-up files.
SET	2.0	11	Sets DOS environment variables.
SETVER	5.0	11	Controls what version number is reported.
SORT	2.0	8	Sorts data forward or backward.
SUBST	3.1	—	Substitutes a string for a pathname.
SYS	1.0	11	Transfers DOS hidden files to a disk.
TIME	1.0	5	Displays and sets the system time.
TREE	2.0	7	Displays directories and filenames.
TYPE	1.0	5	Displays contents of a file.
UNDELETE	5.0	6	Retrieves accidentally deleted files.
UNFORMAT	5.0	—	Restores a disk erased by FORMAT.
VER	2.0	5	Displays the DOS version number.
VERIFY	2.0	—	Verifies all writes to a disk.
VOL	2.0	5	Displays the disk volume label.
XCOPY	3.2	6	Expanded version of the COPY command.

DOS Configuration File Commands

COMMAND	**CHAPTER**	**BRIEF DESCRIPTION OF COMMAND**
BREAK	10	Sets or clears extended Ctrl-Break checking.
BUFFERS	10	Allocates memory for disk buffers.
DEVICE	10	Loads a device driver in the low memory area.
DEVICEHIGH	12	Loads a device driver in the high memory area.
DOS	12	Loads part of DOS in the high memory area.

DRIVPARM	—	Modifies the parameters of an existing drive.
FILES	10	Sets the number of files DOS can access at a time.
LASTDRIVE	—	Specifies the maximum number of disk drives.
SHELL	10	Increases the size of the DOS environment.

DOS Device Driver Commands	**COMMAND**	**CHAPTER**	**BRIEF DESCRIPTION OF COMMAND**
	ANSI.SYS	10	Used to change screens and keyboards.
	DISPLAY.SYS	—	Supports code-page switching for the console.
	DRIVER.SYS	—	Specifies parameters for a nonsupported drive.
	EGA.SYS	12	Restores display when task swapper is used.
	EMM386.EXE	12	Provides access to the upper memory area.
	HIMEM.SYS	12	Manages the use of extended memory.
	PRINTER.SYS	—	Supports code-page switching for printers.
	RAMDRIVE.SYS	10	Creates a RAM disk in memory.
	SMARTDRV.SYS	12	Creates a disk cache in extended memory.

DOS Batch File Commands	**COMMAND**	**CHAPTER**	**BRIEF DESCRIPTION OF COMMAND**
	CALL	13	Executes another batch file.
	ECHO	9	Sets the batch file echo feature on/off.
	FOR	13	Command for repetitive looping.

GOTO	13	Command for branching.
IF	13	Command for conditional branching.
PAUSE	9	Pauses for operator action in a batch file.
REM	9	Provides for remarks in a batch file.

Appendix B
UTILITY SUPPORT PROGRAMS

Numerous utility support programs are available that make DOS easier to use and/or extend its capabilities. These user-friendly programs are usually menu-driven. Some programs are complete DOS command shells that execute DOS commands and their options via menu selections. These are specifically designed to guide users through the process of executing DOS commands, especially in the area of file management. Other utility support programs extend the capabilities of DOS.

Some utility support programs are RAM-resident, which means that they stay in RAM until you need them. They are usually executed by means of a simple combination of keystrokes, even while you are using another program. These programs are also called terminate-and-stay-resident (TSR) programs.

Use of TSR software can be dangerous, especially if you are using more than one TSR program. Unless you load them in the upper memory area, TSR programs can take up valuable space that might be better allocated to the main program. Some programs take so much control of the keyboard that access to your TSR programs can be difficult. Finally, loading TSR programs in the wrong sequence can cause your system to lock up. This problem can often be resolved by shuffling the order.

One word of caution: *Beware of utility programs that you download from an electronic bulletin board or that are given to you by friends.* They may contain a **computer virus** that, once loaded to your system and executed, could cause major problems, such as complete destruction of all your disk files. This appendix lists a sampling of some of the more common and useful utility support programs, along with a brief description of each.

A SAMPLING OF DOS UTILITIES FOR GENERALLY LESS THAN $100

PROGRAM NAME	MAJOR PROGRAM FEATURES
Automenu	Powerful personal menu system.
Check It	System and hardware diagnostics program.
Copy II PC	Backs up protected software.
Crosstalk	Excellent communications facility.
DESQview	Excellent multitasking DOS shell with windows.
Disk Optimizer	Restores fragmented files; includes disk analyzer.
DoubleDOS	Supplements DOS; runs two partitions concurrently.
Fastback Plus	Fast, friendly disk backup program.
FormFiller	Simplifies the completion of preprinted forms.
FormTool Gold	Popular menu-driven form design program.
GOfer	Searches hard disk files for data.
Instant Recall	Personal Information Manager (PIM).
LapLink	Connects a portable computer to another PC.
MS Windows	Mouse-directed DOS shell with multitasking.
Norton Commander	Popular, comprehensive DOS shell.
Norton Utilities	Menu-driven file management and recovery program.
PC Anywhere	Accesses a PC from remote locations.
PC Tools Deluxe	Disk file management, recovery, and backup program.
PK Zip	Data compression and expansion program.
Print Q	Inexpensive print spooler.
ProComm Plus	Powerful communications program.

Q DOS III   Friendly shell that uses sorted and tagged files.

QEMM 386   Popular extended memory manager.

SideKick   Extensive desktop organizer.

Treeview   Powerful, friendly hard disk manager.

ViruScan   Computer virus detection and removal program.

XTree Gold   DOS shell and disk management system.

Appendix C
COMMON DOS ERROR MESSAGES

Abort, Ignore, Retry, Fail?
A disk error has occurred. Enter A to end (abort) the requested task. Enter R to retry the operation if you think that the error might not happen again, or you have corrected the problem (for example, closing the drive latch or reinserting the disk). Press F to end the operation, but continue the requested task. Do *not* enter I, as it can cause a loss of data.

Access denied
You tried to modify a write-protected or read-only file. Modify the file attributes to gain access.

ANSI.SYS must be installed
You tried to execute a command (like MODE) that uses the ANSI.SYS device driver. Install ANSI.SYS in the CONFIG.SYS file and reboot.

Bad command or filename
The command entered is not a valid DOS command, or DOS cannot find the command. Check for correct path.

Bad or missing Command Interpreter
COMMAND.COM is not on the root directory of the boot disk.

Data error reading (or writing) disk
The disk in the specified drive has a bad sector. If entering R (retry) does not resolve the problem, enter A to abort the process.

Directory already exists
You attempted to create a directory using an existing directory name. Use a different name or a different path for the new directory.

Disk unsuitable for system disk
FORMAT detected a bad track on the disk where the system resides. The disk can possibly be formatted as a nonsystem disk.

File allocation table bad

The disk may be defective. Run CHKDSK /F to fix the problem. If the fix is unsuccessful, you must reformat the disk.

File cannot be copied onto itself

The source filename is the same as the target filename. Make sure the filenames, including the disk drive and path, are different.

File creation error

You tried to add a filename that already exists in the directory, or there was not enough space for the file.

File not found

DOS could not find any file(s) that match the name(s) you provided.

Format failure

A fatal disk error prevented DOS from formatting the disk. Try another disk.

Incorrect DOS version

You attempted to run a DOS command from a DOS version different from that used to boot the system. Re-enter the DOS command for the version of DOS that was used to boot the system. Also, see SETVER command.

Insufficient disk space

The disk does not have enough space available to perform the specified operation.

Invalid drive specification

You specified a nonexistent disk drive in a command. Correct the drive identification and re-enter the command.

Invalid media or track 0 bad

Track zero on the disk to be formatted is unusable. Either it is corrupted or the density type is not correct.

Invalid number of parameters

The command line entered did not contain the correct number of parameters for the command invoked. For example, it might have had an extra delimiter.

Invalid parameter(s)

One of the specified command options is wrong or does not exist.

Invalid path, not directory, or directory not empty   You could not remove a directory for one of the specified reasons. Correct the problem and re-enter the command.

Lost allocation units found in chains   The FAT has allocation units marked as used by a file, but there are no directory entries that use those allocation units (see CHKDSK).

Non-system disk or disk error   The default disk is not a bootable DOS disk. If you have a floppy disk in Drive A on a hard disk system, most PCs will boot from the floppy disk.

Not ready error reading disk   DOS cannot read or write to the specified drive. Correct the problem and enter R to retry. If the problem cannot be fixed, enter A to abort the operation.

Path not found   One of the directory names in the path you provided does not exist.

Program too big to fit in memory   DOS cannot load an executable program because of insufficient free space. Remove any unnecessary buffers and TSR programs and try again.

Required parameter missing   You failed to supply a parameter required to execute the command.

Sector not found   DOS was unable to locate all of the sectors for a disk file due to a corrupted File Allocation Table or bad disk (See RECOVER and CHKDSK).

Target diskette may be unusable   The target disk in a DISKCOPY operation has an unrecognizable format or it is defective.

Too many parameters   You supplied too many parameters for a command. Often this is due to extra spaces in a filename.

Write fault error writing device prn   The printer cannot receive data. Make sure the printer is connected (on-line) and in a "ready" status, then press R to retry the operation.

Write protect error

You tried to write data to a disk with a tab covering the write-protect notch, or the disk does not have a notch, which also protects the data it contains.

INDEX